D1443232

SUMMER BERRIES
& AUTUMN FRUITS

Annie Rigg

SUMMER BERRIES & AUTUMN FRUITS

120 sensational, sweet & savory recipes

PHOTOGRAPHY BY TARA FISHER

KYLE BOOKS

To my Mother who finds it impossible
to make just one dessert. *x*

Published in 2016 by Kyle Books
www.kylebooks.com

Distributed by National Book Network
4501 Forbes Blvd, Suite 200,
Lanham, MD 20706
Phone: (800) 462-6420
Fax: (800) 338-4550
customercare@nbnbooks.com

10 9 8 7 6 5 4 3 2 1

ISBN 978-1-909487-43-7

Editor: Judith Hannam
Editorial Assistant: Hannah Coughlin
Copy Editor: Jo Richardson
Designer: Miranda Harvey
Photographer: Tara Fisher
Food and Prop Stylist: Annie Rigg
Production: Nic Jones and Gemma John

Library of Congress Control Number: 2015957117

Color reproduction by ALTA London
Printed and bound in China by 1010 International
Printing Ltd.

Contents

Introduction

Throughout the days, weeks, and months of writing this book my kitchen has been a joy, filled with a constantly changing and seasonal spread of the best available fruit from gardens, farmers markets, specialty suppliers, and growers. And just when I think I've overloaded on one type of fruit, along comes another—overlapping in a way that revitalizes my mind, body, and cooking. Although this book isn't necessarily season specific, it's impossible to ignore the fact that fruit (or any produce for that matter) eaten at optimum ripeness and harvested or picked at its peak is not only better for you, it tastes far superior and is often cheaper. If you are lucky and green-thumbed enough to grow your own produce, then you'll appreciate the thrill of walking to the end of the garden, basket in hand, to select the best of the days offerings—still warm from the sunshine or glistening in rain drops.

In the depths of Winter, when almost all of the native fruits in the US and UK are still a way off, I am glad for the cheering bowl of citrus fruits that greets me in the morning when I venture into the kitchen. Lip puckering grapefruits and oranges both regular and blood, or smaller varieties such as juicy clementines and mandarins, provide a much needed hit of vitamin C to boost the immune system and help keep colds at bay. A large bowl of mixed citrus fruit, cut into neat segments and perhaps adorned with some pomegranate seeds, passion fruit, or blueberries is just the kind of breakfast that one needs on darker days.

As Spring comes knocking my thoughts turn to rhubarb—starting with the almost neon pink hothouse varieties that also make a fantastic breakfast when lightly stewed and served with natural yogurt and a good scattering of granola (homemade if you're of that persuasion). What follows is a profusion of berries with enough variation to keep even the most jaded cook happy. There's preserving to be done, ice cream and sorbets to be made, and light summery cakes and desserts aplenty. On the whole, I prefer to reserve berries for use in sweet cooking but late summer raspberries and blackberries work well with pheasant and other early game.

To spoil us further in the summer months, we are blessed with stone fruits; cherries in colors from blushing pink and yellow to red and deep purple, apricots, plums, and peaches and nectarines with their downy skin. Peaches are possibly one of my favorite fruits, both yellow and white fleshed, round or flat shaped and churned into ice cream, baked into a pie, or sliced and served alongside rich, creamy buffalo mozzarella—or simply eaten by hand with juice dripping down my chin. And I'm not sure anyone can resist a bag full of juicy deep red cherries—always buy double the amount you need for cooking a particular recipe as you'll start eating them before you get home, guaranteed.

Orchard fruits now have a greater significance in my cooking as we have a selection of apple and pear trees in our garden. With my plans to add quince and plum to the mix I'll be finding inventive ways to use what I hope will be a plentiful harvest each autumn. I'm sure that I'll be able to find willing tasters for my apple caramels, and apple pies never fail to please, but I also have an apple press on my wish list for making homemade cider and juice which will no doubt make the most of what can't be cooked with, eaten, or given away.

Throughout the year I take advantage of brightly colored tropical fruit when I can. Mangoes are grown from South America to India, Southeast Asia and beyond, and vary in size, shape, and sweetness. They have thousands of uses and can be diced into salsa and salads, blended into smoothies, lassis, and cocktails. Many tropical fruits pair well with searing hot chiles, salty dressings, and fresh herbs in salads and sauces—the cooling sweetness of the fruit tempering the chile's bite. Melons are plentiful in the summer, and what could be nicer than a plate of wafer-thin slices of salty Parma ham served alongside juicy melon wedges on a hot summer day?

This book is a collection of recipes that reflect the way I like to cook and eat, using fruits that are widely available rather than the obscure and unusual. Within these pages are recipes for preserving including marmalades, jams, curds, and pickles and I have included recipes for drinks—both alcoholic and otherwise. Peach shrub is a new discovery and a recipe that can be adapted to suit other fruits such as berries, apricots, and plums, and although refreshing diluted with soda water, it can be added to your cocktail experiments, perhaps with a dash of bourbon and ginger ale. In each chapter you'll find a wide selection of baking ideas, from crisp wafer cookies for serving with cheese and cakes laden with berries to soufflés, pies, tarts, and donuts. The book is divided into five chapters of fruit varieties and each chapter contains recipes for both sweet and savory dishes that really only scratch the surface of this wonderfully inspiring subject. I wish this book had been four times as long!

I'd like to point out a few notes on commonly used ingredients in my recipes. When using eggs, always use the size stated in a recipe and organic or free-range as a matter of principle. I tend to use sea salt as I feel that this gives a better flavor than regular table salt. I always recommend that you use unsalted butter, particularly for baking, and add salt to taste. With other dry ingredients such as flour, sugar, and chocolate I use the best available or to fit my budget. Dried fruit and nuts should be fresh—which sounds like a contradiction but nuts do have a tendency to turn rancid if well past the use-by dates.

As I write these words, Seville oranges have just started to make an appearance in the stores and I am looking forward to a weekend of marmalade making. Grapefruits are at their juicy best and blood oranges are hot on their heels. I'm already eagerly anticipating what the coming months have to offer from the garden, orchard, and fruit farm.

Citrus

A ray of sunshine in the dark months of winter, a bowl of citrus fruit brings joy to my kitchen and cooking. From leafy little mandarins and clementines to sweet, juicy blood oranges and grapefruit in colors ranging from the palest yellow to nearly crimson—barely a day goes by without me either eating or cooking with citrus fruit in one way or another.

I am constantly dazzled by the variety of dishes that can be created from citrus fruit. They are surely the most varied and versatile of all the fruits, the skin, juice, and flesh all having a myriad of uses with almost nothing going to waste. From preserves, pickles, and drinks to cakes and bakes through to salads, sauces, and dressings, and taking inspiration from all corners of the globe, this subject is worthy of a book all of its own.

I always eat fruit for breakfast and when grapefruits are plentiful during the winter months I can't get enough of them. Skin and segment a mixture of white, pink, and ruby grapefruits and perhaps a couple of blood or regular oranges and add a handful of blueberries, passion fruit, or pomegranate seeds. This breakfast is a real wake-up call for the senses.

The start of the short Seville orange season in December is eagerly awaited by cooks like myself, who scoop up bags of the wrinkly, slightly gnarly fruits whenever they see them. Thick-skinned, loaded with seeds, and not overly pleasant to eat raw, their bitterness and high pectin content are perfect for marmalade making. Blood oranges also have a short season and were originally grown in Italy, Sicily, and Spain. Depending on variety, they are sweeter than normal oranges with a flesh and skin that range in color from being lightly tinged with a pink blush to the Moro variety, that toward the end of the season can have an almost burgundy-colored flesh. They can be used whenever a recipe calls for regular oranges but are especially wonderful in simple jellies, dressings, or juices, where their distinct flavor and color really shine.

Bergamot is another short-seasoned fruit and one that is gaining in popularity and availability. With their pale yellow-colored flesh, not dissimilar to a lemon, these fruits pack a punch with a highly fragrant scent that provides Earl Grey tea with its distinct perfume and makes a wonderful syrup or palate-cleansing sorbet.

If a recipe calls for only the juice of an orange or lemon, remove the peels with a vegetable peeler and either slide them into a jar of granulated sugar to make scented sugar or dry on a baking sheet in a low oven and store in an airtight jar. Two or three strips used in a stew will give it a deeply aromatic citrus note. Or you could make my Orange Bitters on page 14. If you only need half a lemon, slice the remainder, store in a bag in the freezer, and slip a frozen slice or two into a G&T.

When grating zest, always grate the fruit directly over the bowl or pan that you are using to catch any precious oils that are released from the skin. Citrus juice provides an acidic balancing note to dishes, instantly bringing food to life—a squeeze of lemon or lime juice can transform a salad or simple grilled meats and fish.

Bergamot and Mandarin Mini Financiers

The bergamot season is relatively short, so, as with Sevilles, you need to snatch them up when you see them. Bergamots can vary in size and color from that of a small lemon to a large orange, and from yellow to pale green and almost orange, but the moment you press the oils from the skin and breathe in the scent, you'll be certain of what's inside. Bergamots are used to flavor Earl Grey tea and this marmalade variation has the same intense perfume. Tiny delicate morsels such as these seem almost innocent due to their size, but these little cakes pack a punch flavor-wise. If you can't find bergamots, or they are out of season, simply use a large lemon.

MAKES 36 MINI MUFFIN-SIZED CAKES

9 TABLESPOONS UNSALTED BUTTER, DICED, PLUS EXTRA, MELTED, FOR GREASING

⅔ CUP ALL-PURPOSE FLOUR, PLUS EXTRA FOR DUSTING

1¼ CUPS GROUND ALMONDS

1¼ CUPS CONFECTIONERS' SUGAR

¼ TEASPOON BAKING POWDER

1 TABLESPOON FRAGRANT HONEY

FINELY GRATED ZEST OF 1 BERGAMOT

FINELY GRATED ZEST OF 1 MANDARIN

3 LARGE EGG WHITES

A PINCH OF FINE SEA SALT

For the bergamot syrup

JUICE OF 1 BERGAMOT

JUICE OF 2 MANDARINS

¼ CUP GRANULATED SUGAR

Equipment

3 × 12-HOLE MINI MUFFIN PANS OR
1 × 12-HOLE MUFFIN PAN

Preheat the oven to 350°F. Lightly grease the muffin pans with melted butter and dust with a little flour, tapping out the excess.

Sift the flour, ground almonds, confectioners' sugar, and baking powder onto a sheet of parchment paper.

Melt the butter in a small saucepan over low heat, then cook for a couple of minutes until it starts to smell nutty and turns a deep golden brown, swirling the pan to ensure that it browns evenly. Pour into a bowl, add the honey and zests, and let cool slightly.

In a separate bowl, whisk the egg whites with the salt until they hold soft peaks. Add the sifted dry ingredients and fold in using a large metal spoon. Pour the melted butter around the edges of the bowl and carefully fold into the batter, being careful not to knock out too much air. Fill three-quarters of each muffin pan hole and bake on the middle rack of the oven for 10 minutes until well-risen and golden brown.

Meanwhile, combine all the syrup ingredients plus 5 tablespoons of water in a small saucepan and set over low heat to dissolve the sugar. Bring to a gentle simmer and cook until reduced by half.

Let the cakes cool in the pans for 2 minutes, then turn onto a wire rack. Brush the warm cakes with the syrup and leave until cold.

Orange Bitters

Bitters are a wonderful way to add a retro twist to your cocktail making and are firmly back in fashion with the cocktail cognoscenti. Although easy to make at home, you will need to invest in some high-proof vodka, available online or from specialty spirit suppliers, and allow a few weeks for the orange and spices to infuse the spirit. This almost pure vodka is definitely not intended as a mixing vodka and should only be used in small quantities and with caution—in this case, a little really does go a long way. If you are making bitters when Seville oranges are in season, do use them in this recipe, but regular oranges will do.

MAKES 2 CUPS

4 FIRM ORANGES, SCRUBBED IN SOAPY WATER AND DRIED

2 CUPS 88%-BY-VOLUME VODKA (176-PROOF)

1 LARGE CINNAMON STICK, SNAPPED IN HALF

½ VANILLA BEAN

6 GREEN CARDAMOM PODS

1 TEASPOON BLACK PEPPERCORNS

1 TEASPOON FENNEL SEEDS

1 TEASPOON CORIANDER SEEDS

Equipment

LARGE JAR WITH A TIGHT-FITTING LID

COFFEE FILTER OR
CLEAN, FINE CHEESECLOTH

SELECTION OF SMALL BOTTLES

Preheat the oven to 250°F. Remove the peel of each orange using a vegetable peeler—you're after long, thin strips with as little pith as possible. Line a baking sheet with parchment paper and scatter the peel strips on top in a single layer. Place in the oven for 45 minutes to 1 hour until dry but not browned.

Pour the vodka into the large jar and add the dried peels, cinnamon halves, and vanilla bean. Using a mortar and pestle, bruise the cardamom pods to break the skins, then add the other whole spices and give them a light bashing, just enough to break them in half. Add to the vodka, screw the lid on tightly, and give the whole thing a good shake to muddle the flavors.

Leave the jar in a cool, dark spot for 2 weeks but preferably at least 4, and shake the jar once a day. After a couple of days, the orange peels will have begun to impart a wonderful glow to the vodka.

Strain the vodka through either a coffee filter or clean, fine cheesecloth into a jug. Pour into clean small bottles and get creative with cocktails.

Add a drop of orange bitters to a Martini or Champagne cocktail,
or use to pep up a G&T. Or decant into small bottles to give as gifts
to the cocktail enthusiast in your life—just add a note of caution
regarding the alcohol content!

Chocolate Orange Delice

This is a pulling-out-all-the-stops type of recipe—one that takes a little time and requires some skill, but it gives back in terms of impact. Think grown-up, fancy pants Jaffa Cakes.

While I appreciate that this recipe might seem long, in reality it's two for the price of one. You can make it as I suggest or, if you only want petit fours, you could just make the orange *pâte de fruit*. Follow the instructions for that part, pour into a smaller pan (a lined 1-pound loaf pan would work well), leave overnight to set firm, then cut the *pâte* into shapes and toss in granulated or superfine sugar, or dip in melted dark chocolate for a sophisticated spin.

For this recipe I suggest using a chocolate of 68 to 70% cocoa solids. This is my personal preference, and I think it gives a nice balance to the bitter orange, but if your taste is either for something sweeter or more bitter, feel free to use a lower or higher percentage.

SERVES 10 TO 12

For the cake

5 TABLESPOONS UNSALTED BUTTER, SOFTENED, PLUS EXTRA FOR GREASING

¼ CUP GRANULATED SUGAR

¼ CUP CONFECTIONERS' SUGAR

1 MEDIUM EGG, BEATEN

¼ TEASPOON ALMOND EXTRACT

⅓ CUP ALL-PURPOSE FLOUR

¼ TEASPOON BAKING POWDER

¼ CUP GROUND ALMONDS

A PINCH OF SALT

1 TABLESPOON MILK

2½ OUNCES DARK CHOCOLATE, MELTED

For the pâte de fruit layer

3 ORANGES

4 MANDARINS

1¾ CUPS SUPERFINE SUGAR

2 OUNCES APPLE-BASED LIQUID PECTIN (CERTO BRAND)

2 TEASPOONS LEMON JUICE

Continued overleaf...

Start by making the cake: Preheat the oven to 350°F. Grease and line the pan with parchment paper. Cream the butter with both sugars until light and fluffy. Gradually add the beaten egg, a little at a time, beating well between additions and scraping down the sides of the bowl with a rubber spatula. Add the almond extract and mix again. Sift the dry ingredients into the bowl, add the milk, and mix again until smooth. Spoon into the prepared pan, level, and bake on the middle rack of the oven for 9 to 10 minutes, or until pale golden and a wooden skewer comes out clean when inserted into the middle of the cake. Let cool in the pan for 2 to 3 minutes, then, using the parchment paper, carefully transfer to a wire rack and leave until completely cold. Wash the pan, then line the bottom and sides with a sheet of plastic wrap.

Spread the melted chocolate evenly over the top of the cake and let set. Carefully flip the cake back into the lined pan so that the chocolate is now on the underside.

To make the *pâte de fruit* layer, scrub one orange and two mandarins in hot, soapy water to remove any wax or dirt. Place in a saucepan, cover with cold water, and bring to a boil, then simmer gently for 15 minutes until the skins are softened. Drain and let cool for a few minutes.

Cut a thin slice off the top of the softened fruit to remove the stalk end and discard. Cut the fruit into quarters and cut out any seeds and the central pithy core. Coarsely chop the quartered fruit, put into a food processor, and blend until nearly smooth. Push the pulp through a sieve and weigh the resulting purée—you will need about 7 ounces. Squeeze the juice from the remaining fruit—you will need 1½ cups.

Put half the sugar in a medium saucepan and add 2 to 3 tablespoons of water. Set over low heat and dissolve the sugar without stirring.

For the ganache

1 CUP WHIPPING CREAM

3 TABLESPOONS LIGHT BROWN SUGAR

A PINCH OF SALT

8 OUNCES DARK CHOCOLATE,
FINELY CHOPPED

3 TABLESPOONS UNSALTED BUTTER AT
ROOM TEMPERATURE, DICED

For the glaze

3½ OUNCES DARK CHOCOLATE,
FINELY CHOPPED

3 TABLESPOONS UNSALTED BUTTER

3 TABLESPOONS WHOLE MILK

2 TEASPOONS HONEY

2 TABLESPOONS COCOA POWDER

Equipment

8-INCH SQUARE CAKE PAN

SUGAR THERMOMETER

Bring the syrup to a boil and cook until it becomes a deep amber-colored caramel. Off the heat, slowly and carefully add the juice, purée, and remaining sugar. Stir until smooth, then return to low heat to dissolve any hardened caramel. Pop a sugar thermometer into the pan, bring to a steady gentle simmer, and cook until the mixture reaches 225°F. Add the pectin and lemon juice, whisk to combine, then cook until the mixture again reaches 225°F, stirring from time to time. Simmer at this temperature for 2 minutes, stirring frequently. Drop ½ teaspoon of the mixture onto a chilled saucer and leave for about 30 seconds—it should wrinkle when pushed with the tip of your finger. If not, cook for another minute and test again. Slide the pan off the heat and remove the thermometer. Wait for the bubbling to subside, then pour on top of the cake. Leave for at least 2 hours until cold and set firm.

To make the ganache, in a small saucepan, bring the cream to a boil with the sugar and salt. Immediately remove from the heat and pour over the chocolate in a bowl. Mix until smooth and shiny before adding the butter and beating to combine. Pour over the set *pâte de fruit*, spread level with a palette knife, and leave somewhere cool until set firm.

To make the glaze, melt the chocolate and butter with the milk and honey in a small saucepan over low heat, stirring until smooth. Cool for 3 minutes or so before pouring over the ganache. Tap the pan on the work surface to spread level and leave until set before dusting with the cocoa.

To serve, cut into thin slices using a warmed, long-bladed knife.

Blood Orange Granita

A wonderfully refreshing frozen dessert that doesn't require any great skill or an ice-cream maker, granita is the rough, gritty cousin of smooth sorbet or unctuous ice cream.

SERVES 6

1 CUP GRANULATED SUGAR

8 TO 10 BLOOD ORANGES, TO YIELD
2½ TO 3 CUPS JUICE

JUICE OF ½ LEMON

2 TABLESPOONS Campari, PLUS EXTRA
FOR DRIZZLING (BOTH OPTIONAL)

Equipment

LARGE PLASTIC FREEZER-SAFE CONTAINER

Put the sugar in a medium saucepan, add 1 cup of cold water, and bring to a boil. Simmer for 2 minutes, then remove from the heat and let cool to room temperature.

Mix together the orange and lemon juices, and the Campari, if using. Add the sugar syrup and whisk to combine. Pour into the freezer-safe container and freeze for 2 to 3 hours, ensuring it is sitting level. Remove from the freezer and, using a fork, scrape any ice crystals that have formed around the edges of the mixture back into the middle, but do not over-mix—you want large crystals or fine shards. Freeze for another 2 hours and fork the crystals back again. When the whole mixture has frozen, use the fork to scrape the frozen orange syrup into fine, icy shards—it may well double in volume.

Keep frozen until ready to serve, piled into mounds in chilled bowls with perhaps an extra drizzle of Campari.

Bergamot Syrup

Bergamots (sometimes called sweet lemons or bergamotto) are the ugly sisters of the citrus world, with wrinkles and gnarls and an uneven skin tone. But cut one open and they turn into Cinderella. The smell is almost overwhelmingly citrus but with sweet, perfumed undertones, although the juice can be alarmingly bitter and sharp.

This syrup is delicious added to a glass of prosecco or cava for a citrus twist on a kir royale, but can also be made into a rather special sorbet. Simply add the juice of a lemon to half of the syrup and dilute to taste with about 2 cups cold water, then churn in an ice-cream maker according to the manufacturer's instructions.

MAKES ABOUT 1 LITER

6 BERGAMOTS, SCRUBBED IN HOT,
SOAPY WATER AND DRIED

2 CUPS GRANULATED SUGAR

1 BAY LEAF

2 STAR ANISE

Remove the bergamot zest using the fine side of a grater or preferably a Microplane grater if you have one. Cut the fruits in half and press through a juicer—you should aim to have about 1¼ cups of juice but a little over or under is fine.

Put the zest in a saucepan with the sugar, bay leaf, star anise, and 2 cups of cold water and bring slowly to a boil. Simmer gently for 2 to 3 minutes until slightly thickened and then add the juice. Bring back to a simmer and cook for another 2 minutes. Remove from the heat and let cool to room temperature.

Caramelized Mandarin Salad

When we were young, my mother's culinary repertoire for more fancy occasions included a dessert of caramelized oranges, served more often than not with a pile of cream-filled brandy snaps alongside—a true 1970s classic. The oranges were sliced and lay in slightly bitter caramel juice, with crisp caramel shards on top—whether by design or not I was never sure. This is my updated, lighter, and more refreshing version, which wouldn't look out of place on a festive Christmas table. With or without the brandy snaps.

SERVES 4 TO 6

8-10 MANDARINS OR CLEMENTINES—CHOOSE FIRM ONES, WHICH ARE EASIER TO PEEL

¾ CUP SUPERFINE SUGAR

JUICE OF 2 LARGE ORANGES

1 TO 2 TEASPOONS ROSEWATER OR ORANGE FLOWER WATER

SEEDS FROM ½ POMEGRANATE

½ CUP SHELLED PISTACHIOS, COARSELY CHOPPED

2 TO 3 SPRIGS OF MINT, COARSELY CHOPPED

For a more elegant look to the finished salad, rather than using your hands to peel the mandarins, cut a thin slice off the top and bottom of each and sit them upright on the cutting board. Using a sharp, serrated knife, and working from top to bottom, cut the peel away in strips using a sawing action. Try to cut all of the pith away, leaving the fruit in a neat barrel shape. Cut each mandarin in half through the middle and arrange in a serving dish.

To make the caramel, put the sugar in a heavy-bottomed saucepan, add 2 tablespoons of cold water, and set over low to medium heat to dissolve the sugar without stirring. Increase the heat to medium, bring the syrup to a boil, and cook until it becomes amber-colored, swirling the pan to ensure that it cooks evenly.

Meanwhile, heat the orange juice until just below boiling in a separate saucepan or in a bowl in the microwave. Slide the caramel pan off the heat and carefully add the hot juice—the caramel will splutter furiously, so keep your hands covered by a cloth and your face away from the pan. Return to the heat to melt any hardened caramel, bring to a boil, and simmer for 1 minute. Remove from the heat, add the rosewater or orange flower water, and let cool for a few minutes.

Pour the caramel over the mandarins and stir gently to coat the fruit. Leave for 1 hour or so for the caramel to flavor the little oranges and vice versa.

Scatter with the pomegranate seeds, pistachios, and mint and serve.

Cured Citrus Salmon

Since the fish is cured rather than cooked or smoked in this recipe, you will need to source some sparkly, spanking fresh salmon for the best results.

This is an ideal dish to serve as a dinner party appetizer or at a festive meal, as it requires no last-minute cooking or preparation. Serve with a simple salad of lightly pickled cucumber and radishes and perhaps some rye or pumpernickel bread.

SERVES 8

1 LARGE ORANGE

2 LIMES

1 LEMON

3 TABLESPOONS SEA SALT

2 TABLESPOONS GRANULATED SUGAR

1 TEASPOON JUNIPER BERRIES

1 TEASPOON BLACK PEPPERCORNS

1 TEASPOON FENNEL SEEDS

½ TEASPOON CORIANDER SEEDS

1 STAR ANISE

4 TABLESPOONS FINELY CHOPPED DILL

1 WHOLE FILLETED SIDE OF SALMON, SKIN ON, WEIGHING ABOUT 2¼ POUNDS, SCALED AND PIN-BONED

Equipment

2 LARGE, SHALLOW BAKING PANS OR SHEETS

BAG OF FLOUR OR SUGAR, OR A COUPLE OF FOOD CANS, AS WEIGHTS

Cover one pan or baking sheet with a triple thickness of plastic wrap, leaving plenty of excess draping over the sides for wrapping the salmon later.

Wash and dry the citrus fruits and finely grate the zests—if you have a Microplane grater, now is the time to put it to good use. Mix the grated zests with the sea salt and sugar. Lightly crush the juniper berries, peppercorns, and fennel and coriander seeds using a mortar and pestle and add to the salt mix. Break the star anise into small pieces and coarsely grind, then add to the salt mixture with half the chopped dill and mix well.

Scatter one-third of the salt mixture over the middle of the plastic wrap-covered pan. Lay the salmon on top, skin-side down, and cover with the remaining salt mixture, pressing it into the fish with your hands. Tightly wrap the salmon in the plastic wrap and cover with the second pan or sheet topped with weighty food items. Leave the salmon to cure in the fridge for 48 hours.

Unwrap the salmon, scrape off as much of the salt as you can, and pat dry with paper towels. Scatter the salmon with the remaining chopped dill and cut into thin slices with a sharp knife.

Fromage Frais Panna Cotta with Blood Orange Gelatin Dessert

Gelatin dessert and whipped cream. It's a combination that instantly brings to mind children's parties—available in any color and flavor of the rainbow. This version, however, is more suited to adults. The contrast between refreshing blood orange gelatin dessert and the cool, slightly tangy panna cotta not only looks rather beautiful but is quite delicious too, especially when served with the Orange and Anise Biscotti on page 29.

SERVES 8

For the gelatin dessert

3 SHEETS OF PLATINUM-GRADE
LEAF GELATIN

ABOUT 8 BLOOD ORANGES,
TO YIELD 2 CUPS JUICE

2 TABLESPOONS SUPERFINE SUGAR,
OR TO TASTE

For the panna cotta

½ VANILLA BEAN (OR 1 TEASPOON VANILLA
BEAN PASTE)

1½ CUPS HEAVY CREAM

½ CUP SUPERFINE SUGAR

1 STRIP OF PEEL FROM A LEMON

4 SHEETS OF PLATINUM-GRADE
LEAF GELATIN

2¼ CUPS FROMAGE FRAIS

Start by making the gelatin dessert: Soak the gelatin sheets in a bowl of cold water for 10 minutes to soften. In a small saucepan, bring ½ cup of the orange juice and the sugar to just below boiling point over medium heat. Stir to dissolve the sugar, then remove from the heat. Drain the gelatin and squeeze out any excess water—I also like to blot it quickly on a clean kitchen towel or paper towels. Add to the hot juice and whisk until it has melted. Pour into a pitcher, add the remaining orange juice, and whisk again. Taste for sweetness, adding a little more sugar if needed. Divide the jelly between eight glasses, arrange on a tray, and slide into the fridge to chill and set firm—this will take at least 2 hours.

Now make the panna cotta: If using the vanilla bean, slit it down its length with the tip of a sharp knife and scrape the seeds into a small saucepan, then add the empty pod to the pan (or just add the vanilla paste). Add the cream, sugar, and lemon peel and bring slowly to just below boiling point, then remove from the heat and leave for 20 minutes to infuse. Meanwhile, soak the gelatin sheets in a bowl of cold water for about 10 minutes to soften.

Return the infused cream to just below boiling point. Drain the gelatin and quickly blot dry before whisking into the cream. Add the fromage frais and whisk until smooth, then strain into a pitcher. Let cool slightly, then carefully pour over the set gelatin. Cover the glasses with plastic wrap and leave in the fridge for about 4 hours or until set.

Orange and Anise Biscotti

I really love these elegant, wafer-thin biscotti, which almost melt in the mouth and are ideal to serve alongside creamy desserts, sorbets, or simply with vin santo and/or coffee. The uncooked mixture is softer than one would expect for biscotti, hence the need to bake it in a loaf pan rather than free-form, as is usual.

MAKES ABOUT 60

BUTTER, FOR GREASING

1 CUP BLANCHED ALMONDS

4 LARGE EGGS

1 CUP GRANULATED SUGAR

FINELY GRATED ZEST OF 1 LARGE ORANGE

1 TEASPOON VANILLA EXTRACT

1 TO 2 TEASPOONS LIGHTLY CRUSHED ANISE SEEDS

3 CUPS ALL-PURPOSE FLOUR

1 TEASPOON BAKING POWDER

½ TEASPOON BAKING SODA

A GOOD PINCH OF SEA SALT

Equipment
2 × 2-POUND LOAF PANS

Preheat the oven to 350°F. Grease and line the bottom and sides of the loaf pans with parchment paper.

Put the almonds on a baking sheet and lightly toast in the oven for 4 minutes until pale golden. Cool and coarsely chop.

Whisk the eggs with the sugar for 2 to 3 minutes until light and foamy. Add the orange zest, vanilla, and anise and whisk to combine. Sift the flour, baking powder, baking soda, and salt into the bowl, add the toasted almonds, and combine.

Divide the dough in half, spoon into the prepared pans, spread level, and bake on the middle rack of the oven for about 30 minutes until risen, firm, and golden. Let cool in the pans for 10 minutes, then turn onto a wire rack and leave until completely cold. Reduce the oven temperature to 300°F.

Using a long, serrated bread knife, cut each loaf into slices no thicker than 1/16 inch and arrange on parchment paper-covered baking sheets. Bake in batches on the middle rack for 15 to 20 minutes until crisp and very lightly toasted, swapping the pans around so that they cook evenly. Remove and cool on wire racks before serving. They will keep for up to 1 week in an airtight box.

Lemon and Poppy Seed Madeleines

This is a multi-cultural bake if ever there was one, with a nod to France from whence the buttery madeleine originated, a wink to the US and Eastern Europe for the addition of poppy seeds, and a cheeky grin to Great Britain for the nifty use of lemon curd. Madeleine pans can vary in size and shape, so the number of cakes that you'll get from this recipe will vary according to whatever pan you're using. They are best eaten on the day of making.

MAKES ABOUT 20

10 TABLESPOONS UNSALTED BUTTER

1⅓ CUPS ALL-PURPOSE FLOUR, PLUS EXTRA FOR DUSTING

1 TEASPOON BAKING POWDER

1 TABLESPOON POPPY SEEDS, PLUS EXTRA FOR SCATTERING

3 LARGE EGGS

¾ CUP GRANULATED SUGAR

A PINCH OF SEA SALT

FINELY GRATED ZEST OF 1 LEMON

12–15 TEASPOONS LEMON CURD (SEE PAGE 33 FOR HOMEMADE)

For the lemon glaze

JUICE OF ½ LEMON

1¼ CUPS CONFECTIONERS' SUGAR, PLUS EXTRA IF NEEDED

Equipment

2 × 12-HOLE MADELEINE PANS

Melt the butter and use a little to grease the inside of the madeleine pans, ensuring that you get it into every groove and corner. Dust with a little flour, tapping out the excess, then pop in the fridge while you prepare the batter.

Sift the flour and baking powder together in a bowl, stir in the poppy seeds, and set aside.

In the bowl of a mixer fitted with the whisk attachment (or using a hand-held mixer), beat the eggs, sugar, and salt for about 5 minutes (longer if using a hand-held mixer) until thick, pale, and doubled in volume. Add the zest and mix to combine.

Using a large metal spoon and a figure-eight action, fold in the sifted dry ingredients. Carefully pour the melted butter around the edges of the bowl and fold in. Cover the bowl with plastic wrap and chill for 30 minutes while you preheat the oven to 375°F.

Drop a rounded teaspoon of batter into the middle of each madeleine indentation and gently spread to fill, leaving a little dip in the middle. Spoon a scant teaspoonful of lemon curd into the dip and cover with a little more batter. Bake on the middle rack of the oven for about 12 minutes until well-risen and golden.

Meanwhile, prepare the glaze: Whisk together the lemon juice and confectioners' sugar until smooth. You want the glaze to be thick enough to just coat the back of a spoon, so add more sugar or a drop of water to adjust the consistency if necessary.

Turn the madeleines onto a wire rack, let cool for a couple of minutes, and then brush with a little glaze and finish with a light scattering of poppy seeds.

Lemon Curd

Homemade lemon curd is one of the most delicious things you can possibly make, and once you've done so, you'll never buy a jar of pre-made again. It's a ray of sunshine in a jar and, as it uses only a few simple ingredients that you're likely to have in your kitchen, it can be rustled up at a moment's notice. But as with all simple dishes, the secret to its success lies in using the best possible ingredients you can lay your hands on: the lemons need to be fresh and firm; the butter unsalted and preferably organic; and the eggs should come from the happiest chickens you can find—not only will they taste superior but the color of the yolks is often deeper, resulting in an even more vibrant curd. Once you've discovered the delights of making lemon curd, you could try adding passion fruit pulp or lime zest and juice in place of half of the lemon.

MAKES ABOUT 3 JARS

FINELY GRATED ZEST AND JUICE OF
4 LEMONS

2 LARGE ORGANIC EGGS

3 LARGE ORGANIC EGG YOLKS

1 CUP GRANULATED SUGAR

9 TABLESPOONS UNSALTED BUTTER, DICED

A PINCH OF SALT

Equipment

3 × 12-OUNCE CANNING JARS

Put the lemon zest and juice into a heatproof glass or ceramic bowl. Add the whole eggs and yolks and whisk to break up the eggs. Add the sugar, butter, and salt, and whisk to combine. Set the bowl over a saucepan of simmering water, but don't allow the bottom of the bowl to come into contact with the simmering water, otherwise you'll end up with scrambled eggs rather than silky smooth curd. Stir frequently until the butter has melted and the sugar has dissolved.

Continue to cook for about 10 minutes, stirring often, until the curd is hot to the touch and has thickened enough to coat the back of the spoon and will hold a wobbly ribbon trail when the spoon is lifted from the bowl.

Remove from the heat and pass the curd through a fine-mesh sieve into a pitcher or bowl. Pour into sterilized jars (see page 132) and leave until completely cold before screwing on the lids and chilling. It will keep for up to 10 days in the fridge.

The uses for lemon curd are endless—serve with scones and
cream, as a filling for little pastry tarts, madeleines (see page 30),
and Victoria cakes, piped into donuts, layered in
a trifle, stirred into yogurt, folded through ice cream,
rolled into roulade, as a topping for meringue… or simply
spooned from the jar.

Orange Curd

I like to use a mixture of Seville oranges and regular oranges, and perhaps add a couple of clementines or mandarins into the mix when they are in season.

MAKES 1 LARGE JAR

3 TO 4 ORANGES SCRUBBED IN HOT, SOAPY
WATER AND DRIED

2 LARGE ORGANIC EGGS

2 LARGE ORGANIC EGG YOLKS

⅔ CUP GRANULATED SUGAR

5 TABLESPOONS UNSALTED BUTTER, DICED

A PINCH OF SALT

1 TEASPOON LEMON JUICE

Equipment

1 × 14-OUNCE CANNING JAR

Finely grate the zest from three of the oranges and place two-thirds in a heatproof glass or ceramic bowl, setting aside the remaining grated zest for later. Squeeze the juice into a glass measuring cup— you're going to need ¾ cup, and any left over is the cook's perk and should be poured into a glass and drunk immediately (unless you're using Seville oranges, in which case it's likely to be too bitter).

Add the juice to the zest in the bowl, then continue making the curd following the method for Lemon Curd (see page 33). Once the curd has thickened to the required consistency, mix in the lemon juice to lift and balance the flavors. Add the reserved grated zest once the curd has been strained. Continue as before but using one large sterilized jar.

Ruby Grapefruit Curd

Don't be fooled into thinking that ruby grapefruit juice will yield a blushing pink curd—it's the yolks that give curds most of their color. But if you wanted to perk up the pinkness of the curd, you could add a tiny drop of pink food coloring paste. Although it's mighty fine as it is, you can flavor this tangy curd with many things, such as vanilla seeds, grated fresh ginger, pink or black peppercorns, and star anise. Simply add to the juice as it's reducing.

MAKES 1 LARGE JAR

3 RUBY OR PINK GRAPEFRUITS, SCRUBBED IN
HOT, SOAPY WATER AND DRIED

2 LARGE ORGANIC EGGS

2 LARGE ORGANIC EGG YOLKS

⅔ CUP GRANULATED SUGAR

5 TABLESPOONS UNSALTED BUTTER, DICED

A PINCH OF SALT

1 TEASPOON LEMON JUICE

Equipment

1 × 14-OUNCE CANNING JAR

Finely grate the zest from two of the grapefruits and place in a heatproof ceramic or glass bowl. Squeeze the juice from all three and pour into a glass measuring pitcher—you'll need 1¼ cups, and any left over should be, in my opinion, chilled and mixed into an early evening cocktail, perhaps with a dash of bourbon and lots of ice. Pour the juice into a small saucepan, bring to a boil over medium heat, and reduce by half. Let cool for 10 minutes.

Add the cooled juice to the zest in the bowl, then continue making the curd following the instructions for Lemon Curd (see page 33). Once the curd has thickened to the required consistency, mix in the lemon juice to lift and balance the flavors. Continue as before but using one large sterilized jar.

Lime Marshmallows with Passion Fruit Sherbet

Homemade marshmallows are really something special—my niece calls them "dreamy" and has vowed never to eat store bought again! These light, sugary puffs have a hit of lime and an added oopmh of passion fruit sherbert to dip into. Freeze-dried passion fruit powder is available in specialty grocers or online.

MAKES ABOUT 30

SUNFLOWER OIL, FOR OILING

2 TABLESPOONS CONFECTIONERS' SUGAR

2 TABLESPOONS CORNSTARCH

6 SHEETS OF PLATINUM-GRADE LEAF GELATIN

2 LARGE EGG WHITES

A PINCH OF SALT

1¾ CUPS SUPERFINE SUGAR

1 TABLESPOON LIQUID GLUCOSE OR CORN SYRUP

FINELY GRATED ZEST OF 2 LIMES AND JUICE OF 1

For the passion fruit sherbet

½ CUP GRANULATED SUGAR

½ TEASPOON CITRIC ACID

¼ TEASPOON BAKING SODA

1 TABLESPOON FREEZE-DRIED PASSION FRUIT POWDER (AVAILABLE ONLINE OR IN SPECIALTY GROCERS)

Equipment

8-INCH SQUARE BAKING PAN

SUGAR THERMOMETER

Lightly oil the baking pan, line with plastic wrap or parchment paper, and lightly oil this as well. Mix the confectioners' sugar and cornstarch together in a small bowl or freezer bag and dust the lined pan with an even coating. Pour any excess back into the bag or bowl and reserve.

Soak the gelatin sheets in a bowl of cold water for 10 minutes until soft. Place the egg whites in the bowl of a mixer fitted with a whisk attachment and add the salt and 1 tablespoon of the superfine sugar but don't start mixing just yet.

Put the remaining sugar and glucose or corn syrup in a medium saucepan and add ⅔ cup cold water. Place the pan over medium heat and stir gently to dissolve the sugar. Increase the heat, pop the sugar thermometer into the pan, and bring the mixture to a boil. Cook at a steady boil until the syrup reaches 250°F. Remove from the heat.

At this point, speed and concentration are important. Drain the gelatin and blot with a clean kitchen towel or paper towels. Whisk the egg whites until they hold stiff peaks. Add the gelatin to the hot syrup and stir until completely melted. With the motor running on medium speed, add the syrup to the egg whites in a steady stream. Add the lime juice and continue to whisk for about 6 minutes until the mixture is cool, very glossy white, and stiff enough to hold a firm ribbon trail when the whisk is lifted from the bowl. Add the lime zest and mix well.

Scoop the marshmallow into the prepared pan and spread level with a palette knife. Let set in a cool place for at least 4 hours.

Meanwhile, put all the sherbet ingredients into the bowl of a food processor and blend for 1 to 2 minutes until finely ground.

Put the reserved confectioners' sugar mixture onto a large baking sheet. Turn the marshmallow out of the pan onto the baking sheet, peel off the lining paper, and cut the marshmallow into squares using a greased kitchen knife. Serve with a good sprinkling of the sherbet, plus extra for dipping.

Citrus Marmalade

I'm not going to lie, marmalade making takes time, but it's a small investment to make for the benefit of having a stash of homemade preserves that will last throughout the year and give you great pleasure each morning at your breakfast table. Cutting peel into shreds is somewhat labor intensive, but it's hardly back-breaking stuff and you could either draft in willing helpers or do as I do and put the radio on and listen to something soothing while rhythmically chopping away. My preference is for a marmalade that is less bitter and with a finer shred, and this really hits the spot. The combination of fruits produces a slightly sweeter, lighter preserve than one made purely from Seville oranges.

MAKES ABOUT 8 JARS

2 SEVILLE ORANGES

3 TANGERINES

1 GRAPEFRUIT

1 LEMON

8¾ CUPS PRESERVING OR GRANULATED SUGAR

Equipment

LARGE STAINLESS STEEL PRESERVING PAN

CLEAN CHEESECLOTH SQUARE AND KITCHEN STRING

8 × 16-OUNCE CANNING JARS

JAM FUNNEL (OPTIONAL)

You will need a combined weight of 2 to 2¼ pounds fruit. Wash and dry all the fruit, cut in half, squeeze the juice, and pour into a large, stainless steel preserving pan. Gather up any seeds that have collected in the juicer.

Cut each citrus shell in half again and, using a teaspoon, scrape out the seeds and membrane, put with the other seeds, tie up tightly in the cheesecloth, then suspend into the preserving pan by tying to the handle.

Using a sharp knife, shred the citrus peel. I like marmalade with finely shredded peels, but if you're of the more chunky persuasion, then please feel free to shred accordingly. Put all the peels in the pan, along with 8 cups of cold water, cover, and set aside to soak overnight or for at least 12 hours.

The next day, bring the contents of the pan slowly to a boil over medium heat. Reduce the heat, half cover the pan, and simmer gently for about 1 hour, or until the peels are very soft and can be squashed when pressed between your fingers. This is a very important as, once the sugar is added, the peels will not soften any further.

Preheat the oven to 300°F. Put the sugar in a heatproof bowl and warm in the oven for 10 minutes. Pop two saucers into the fridge ready to test for a set. Meanwhile, sterilize the jars (see note on page 132).

Remove the cheesecloth bag and set aside on a plate until cool enough to handle. Squeeze the pectin-filled juice from the cheesecloth bag into the pan and discard the bag.

Add the warmed sugar and stir gently until dissolved. Bring to a boil and continue to cook at a steady rolling boil for about 30 minutes until setting point has been reached. Start testing for set after 15 minutes: Drop a teaspoonful of the preserve onto one of the chilled saucers, leave it for 30 seconds, and then push the preserve with the tip of your finger. If it wrinkles, it's ready; if not, cook for another 5 minutes and test again. Test every 5 minutes until setting point has been reached.

Once the marmalade has reached setting point, remove the pan from the heat, scoop off any foam with a slotted spoon, and let the marmalade cool for about 10 minutes. If you bottle it without cooling, the peels will rise to the top rather than be evenly distributed.

Pour or ladle into a pitcher and pour into the warm, sterilized jars, leaving ¼ to ½ inch of headspace. Wipe the jars to remove any drips, tightly seal with lids, and process in a water bath (see page 40). Leave until completely cold before labeling. Store in a cool, dark cupboard for up to 1 year and up to 3 months in the fridge after opening.

Seville Orange Marmalade with Whisky and Ginger

Your window of opportunity for making real marmalade using Seville oranges is pretty small—availability in the US from specialty stores is generally December to March, weather and harvest depending, so seize the fruit and the moment! If you happen to have some candied ginger in your cupboards, then finely chop a couple of nuggets and add to the pan with the whisky for an extra ginger hit.

MAKES ABOUT 8 JARS

2¼ POUNDS SEVILLE ORANGES

1 LEMON

2-INCH PIECE OF FRESH GINGER

10 CUPS PRESERVING OR GRANULATED SUGAR

¼ CUP WHISKY OR GINGER WINE

Equipment

LARGE STAINLESS STEEL PRESERVING PAN

CLEAN CHEESECLOTH SQUARE AND KITCHEN STRING

8 × 16-OUNCE CANNING JARS

JAM FUNNEL (OPTIONAL)

Before starting, give the oranges a good scrub in hot soapy water to clean. Cut each fruit in half and squeeze out all of the juice. Any seeds and pith that gather in the juicer should be poured into a bowl and set aside. Pour the resulting juice, and that from the lemon too, into a large stainless steel preserving pan.

Follow the method given for the Citrus Marmalade on page 39 in steps 2 and 3 to prepare the orange peels, then put in the preserving pan and cover with 8½ cups of cold water. Peel and finely shred the ginger, then add to the preserving pan. Mix well, cover, and set aside for 24 hours.

The next day, again follow the method for cooking the Citrus Marmalade from step 4 onward. Start testing for a set after 30 minutes, and once it has reached setting point, add the whisky or ginger wine to the pan and boil for another 30 seconds, then remove the pan from the heat. Let cool and then bottle and store as before.

For tips on how to process in a water bath and other canning guidelines, consult the USDA guidelines for food safety and best practices (nchfp.uga.edu), and note that processing times will vary depending on your altitude and the size of the jars you use.

Bergamot Preserve

As this preserve is unusual, I like to bottle it into smaller jars than normal to make a rather special gift.

MAKES 4 SMALL JARS

1½ POUNDS BERGAMOTS (5 OR 6 FRUITS)

2 SWEET ORANGES

7½ CUPS PRESERVING OR GRANULATED SUGAR

Equipment

STAINLESS STEEL PRESERVING PAN

CLEAN CHEESECLOTH SQUARE
AND KITCHEN STRING

4 × 9-OUNCE CANNING JARS

JAM FUNNEL (OPTIONAL)

Scrub the fruit in hot soapy water to clean. Remove the zest from half of the bergamots using a vegetable peeler and cut into fine shreds. Cut all of the fruit in half, squeeze the juice, and pour into a preserving pan. Scoop the seeds and any pithy membrane from the juicer and the shells of the squeezed-out fruits onto a square of clean cheesecloth. Tie it up tightly, then suspend into the preserving pan by tying to the handle. Add 7½ cups of cold water, cover, and set aside for 24 hours to soften the peels.

The next day, follow the method given for Citrus Marmalade on page 39 from step 4 onward. Store in a cool, dark cupboard for up to 6 months and in the fridge after opening.

Orange and Beet Salad

For many years my family lived in South West France, and during the summer months we ate nearly every meal outside under a walnut tree in the garden. Lunches often came in the form of salads prepared by my stepfather and were composed from whatever was good that day in his vegetable garden. The salads were arranged as little piles of ingredients on large plates with often up to ten different items, and this is my slightly smaller take on that. Oranges are wonderful when combined with beets, bitter salad leaves, and wafer-thin slices of salty air-dried ham. Feel free to add as many other elements to this salad as you feel fit or have on hand—thinly sliced fennel, radishes, and crisp French beans would all be delicious. The only thing missing is the French sunshine.

SERVES 4 TO 6

6 SMALL BEETS

SALT AND FRESHLY GROUND BLACK PEPPER

6 TABLESPOONS EXTRA VIRGIN OLIVE OIL

2 TABLESPOONS SHERRY VINEGAR

1 SMALL GARLIC CLOVE, CRUSHED

4 ORANGES

2 HEADS OF RED CHICORY

2 HEADS OF WHITE CHICORY

BUNCH OF DANDELION (PISENLIT) LEAVES

½ CUP PECANS, COARSELY CHOPPED

2 TABLESPOONS SNIPPED CHIVES

12 SLICES OF AIR-DRIED HAM

Cook the unpeeled beets in a medium saucepan of salted boiling water for about 20 minutes, depending on size, until tender when tested with the tip of a knife. Drain and peel while still warm. Cut into quarters (or slimmer wedges if on the large side) and transfer into a bowl.

In a small bowl, whisk together the olive oil, sherry vinegar, garlic, and a good seasoning of salt and black pepper. Drizzle 1 to 2 tablespoons of the dressing over the warm beets and leave until cold.

Cut a thin slice off the top and bottom of each orange so that they sit upright on the cutting board. Using a small, sharp serrated knife and a sawing action, working from the top to the bottom, cut the peel and all the pith away from the fruit in strips all the way around. You should end up with denuded barrel-shaped oranges. Cut each segment away from the orange membrane and into a bowl.

Separate the chicory and dandelion leaves, wash in cold water, and dry on a clean kitchen towel. Divide between serving plates and add a pile of beets and orange segments. Scatter with the pecans and chives and drizzle with the dressing. Drape the slices of air-dried ham alongside, season with salt and black pepper, and serve.

Orange-scented Churros with Caramel Orange Chocolate Sauce

What's not to love about churros? Crisp, fried dough strips, tossed in sugar and served while still warm with a rich chocolate dipping sauce... only these ones are better! They have a hint of orange zest and a smattering of grated chocolate in the mix. The orange theme continues in a caramel chocolate fashion for the dipping sauce.

SERVES 4 TO 6

For the churros batter

7 TABLESPOONS UNSALTED BUTTER, DICED

A GOOD PINCH OF SEA SALT

1⅓ CUPS ALL-PURPOSE FLOUR

¼ TEASPOON BAKING POWDER

3 LARGE EGGS, LIGHTLY BEATEN

1 TEASPOON ORANGE FLOWER WATER

FINELY GRATED ZEST OF 1 ORANGE

6 CUPS SUNFLOWER OIL, FOR DEEP-FRYING

1½ OUNCES DARK CHOCOLATE, COARSELY GRATED

1 CUP GRANULATED SUGAR

For the chocolate sauce

⅔ CUP SUPERFINE SUGAR

FRESHLY SQUEEZED JUICE OF 2 ORANGES

⅔ CUP HEAVY CREAM

3½ OUNCES DARK CHOCOLATE, FINELY CHOPPED

1 TEASPOON UNSALTED BUTTER

A GOOD PINCH OF SEA SALT

Equipment

SUGAR THERMOMETER

LARGE PIPING BAG FITTED WITH A LARGE STAR NOZZLE

Place the butter in a medium saucepan, add ¾ cup of cold water and the sea salt, and set over low heat until the butter has melted. Meanwhile, sift the flour and baking powder onto a sheet of parchment paper. Bring the water and butter mixture to a rolling boil and then immediately remove from the heat. Working quickly, pour the dry ingredients into the pan and beat vigorously with a wooden spoon until the mixture comes away from the sides of the pan in a smooth, glossy mass. Transfer to a bowl and let cool for 3 to 4 minutes.

Gradually add the beaten eggs to the batter, mixing well after each addition, until the mixture is smooth, glossy, and drops reluctantly from the spoon. Add the orange flower water and orange zest and mix to combine. Cover the bowl with a clean kitchen towel and let cool to room temperature.

Meanwhile, make the sauce: In a small, heavy-bottomed saucepan, heat the sugar with 1 to 2 tablespoons of hot water over low heat without stirring until dissolved. Bring to a boil and cook until the syrup becomes amber-colored. Take off the heat and add the juice—the caramel will hiss and splutter and may well harden in the pan. Return to low heat to re-melt it. Once it's silky smooth, add the cream and heat to just below boiling point. Remove from the heat, add the chocolate, butter, and sea salt, and stir until smooth.

Pour the sunflower oil into a large, wide sauté pan and place over medium heat. Heat the oil to 350°F. Stir the grated chocolate into the batter, then scoop into the piping bag. Pour the sugar onto a large baking sheet and line another with a double or triple thickness of paper towels. Pipe four long fingers of batter directly into the hot oil, cutting off each strip with scissors. Don't crowd the pan, as this will lower the oil temperature, resulting in soggy, oily, and heavy churros. Cook for about 45 seconds on each side until golden brown and crisp. Remove with a slotted spoon and drain on the paper towels. Roll the warm churros in the sugar and serve immediately with the warm chocolate sauce. Ensure the oil comes back up to temperature before cooking the next batch.

Portuguese Lemon Tarts

My *pastel de nata*, or custard tarts, aren't quite classic, as they are laced with lemon, but hopefully they are simpler to make. The pastry dough, which is similar to puff, takes a bit of forward planning and needs to be started the day before you plan to bake. Nothing, in my opinion, compares to homemade, but if you're short on time, then store-bought all-butter puff pastry would make an acceptable substitute. They are best eaten on the day of making.

MAKES 20 TO 24

For the dough

2¼ CUPS ALL-PURPOSE FLOUR, PLUS EXTRA FOR DUSTING

A GOOD PINCH OF SEA SALT

12 TABLESPOONS UNSALTED BUTTER, SOFTENED

For the filling

1½ CUPS WHOLE MILK

JUICE OF 2 LEMONS

FINELY GRATED ZEST OF 1 LEMON

1¼ CUPS GRANULATED SUGAR

4 LEVEL TABLESPOONS CORNSTARCH

6 LARGE EGG YOLKS

Equipment

2 × 12-HOLE MUFFIN PANS OR SIMILAR-SIZED INDIVIDUAL PIE PANS

Start by making the dough: Pour the flour into a mixing bowl, add the salt and ¾ cup cold water, and mix until you have an almost smooth dough. Lightly dust the work surace with flour, remove the dough from the bowl, and knead very briefly until smooth. Pat into a square, cover with an upturned bowl, and let rest for 15 minutes.

Lightly dust the work surface with flour again and roll the dough into a neat rectangle three times as long as it is wide (about 18 × 6 inches) and with one of the shorter sides nearest to you. Mentally divide the rectangle of dough into thirds—each third a rough square shape—and spread 9 tablespoons of the butter evenly over the middle third. Fold the bottom third up to cover the butter and the top third down to make a neat square shape. Turn the dough 90 degrees clockwise so that the open flap side

is now on the left. Roll into a rectangle again and fold the bottom third up into the middle and the top third down again. Carefully wrap with plastic wrap and chill for 1 hour.

Lightly dust the work surface with flour and again roll out the dough into a rectangle (about 18 × 6 inches). Fold and roll the dough as before, then chill again for 1 hour.

Lightly dust the work surface once again and roll out the dough into a neat rectangle about 16 × 20 inches. Spread the remaining butter over the surface, being careful not to tear the dough. Starting at the edge closest to you, roll the dough into a tight spiral log, trim the ends, and cut the log in half to make handling easier. Wrap each log in plastic wrap and chill for about 4 hours or overnight until firm.

Meanwhile, in a saucepan, bring the milk, ⅔ cup cold water, and the lemon juice slowly to just below boiling point. In a bowl, whisk the lemon zest with the sugar, cornstarch, and egg yolks. Pour in half the milk mixture, whisk until smooth, then return to the pan and cook over low heat, whisking constantly, until it has thickened and no longer tastes of cornstarch. Remove from the heat, pour into a clean bowl, and cover the surface with plastic wrap to prevent a skin from forming. Let cool, then chill until needed.

Preheat the oven to 400°F. Lightly dust the work surface with flour and cut the dough logs into ½-inch thick slices. Roll out each one to a thin disc about 4 inches across. Press the dough into the pans so that it comes up the sides. Don't worry about trimming off the edges. Scoop a rounded teaspoonful of the custard into each hole. Bake on the middle rack of the oven for about 25 minutes until the filling is tinged with brown and the dough is crisp and golden. Leave in the pans for 5 to 10 minutes, then transfer to a wire rack until cold.

Slow-cooked Lamb Shoulder with Oranges

I love food like this—something that is utterly delicious and takes little effort but relies heavily on the quality of the ingredients used. In this case, a good hunk of lamb, marinated with aromatic flavorings and slow-cooked to the point of melting. It benefits from overnight marinating, but is the kind of dish that you can pop in the oven and go for a long walk without worrying about it coming to any harm. There's no need to make gravy either—the onions and oranges produce a delicious pan juice that is perfect served with a pile of crunchy fennel seed potatoes or fluffy herby couscous.

SERVES 4 TO 6

1 HEAPING TEASPOON CUMIN SEEDS

1 HEAPING TEASPOON FENNEL SEEDS

2 SMALL DRIED RED CHILES

1 TEASPOON ANCHO CHILE POWDER OR SMOKED PAPRIKA

3 TABLESPOONS OLIVE OIL

3 TABLESPOONS HONEY

SALT AND FRESHLY GROUND BLACK PEPPER

4½-POUND LAMB SHOULDER ON THE BONE

4 TO 5 SMALL RED ONIONS, QUARTERED

2 SEVILLE OR BITTER ORANGES, SCRUBBED IN HOT, SOAPY WATER AND DRIED, THEN QUARTERED

2 HEADS OF GARLIC, HALVED HORIZONTALLY

1 CINNAMON STICK

2 TABLESPOONS POMEGRANATE MOLASSES

Spoon the cumin and fennel seeds and dried chiles into a small, dry frying pan and place over low to medium heat for a minute or so until they start to smell aromatic, shaking the pan so that they toast evenly. Lightly grind the toasted spices using a mortar and pestle—don't reduce them to a powder. Add the chile powder or smoked paprika, olive oil, honey, and a seasoning of sea salt and black pepper.

Using a sharp knife, cut 5 to 6 slashes into the lamb shoulder, to allow the aromatic flavors to really penetrate the meat. Place the lamb in a large freezer bag (or roasting pan if you find this easier) and rub the spice mixture into the meat. Then add the onions, oranges, garlic, and cinnamon stick. Massage everything together so that the meat is really well basted, seal the bag (or cover the meat well if it's in a roasting pan), and chill overnight. The next day, bring the lamb back to room temperature and preheat the oven to 375°F.

Put everything in a large roasting pan, making sure the lamb is skin-side up, and that there is an even distribution of onions, oranges, and garlic around the meat. Cook, uncovered, for 20 minutes, then cover the roasting pan tightly with foil, reduce the heat to 300°F, and cook for another 2½ hours until the lamb is tender. Remove the foil and return the heat to 375°F. Spoon the pomegranate molasses over the meat, baste with the pan juices, and cook for another 20 minutes until the lamb is nicely browned and sticky.

Let the lamb rest in the pan, covered with foil, for a good 20 minutes before pulling the meat from the bone using forks and serving with the pan juices poured over.

Spring Salad with Lemon Dressing and Goat Cheese Toasts

I use this lemony dressing for all kinds of salads—it goes beautifully with tomatoes and basil, grilled zucchini and eggplant, sliced avocados, or a simple leaf salad. Gremolata is a classic garnish for osso bucco, but it's also another workhorse recipe—scatter it over grilled meats, grilled vegetable salads, risotto, or grilled fish for an instant lift. Try to buy peas and fava beans still in the pod rather than prepared, or if you are lucky enough to grow your own, use these—they'll be fresher and more flavorful.

SERVES 4 AS AN APPETIZER OR
LIGHT LUNCH

A LARGE BUNCH OF ASPARAGUS

1¼ CUPS SHELLED PEAS

1¼ CUPS SHELLED FAVA BEANS

2½ CUPS BABY LEAF SPINACH

A HANDFUL OF PEA SHOOTS

4 SLICES OF SOURDOUGH BREAD

7 OUNCES ASH-COVERED YOUNG GOAT
CHEESE LOG

For the gremolata

2 GARLIC CLOVES, FINELY CHOPPED

¼ CUP FINELY CHOPPED
FLAT-LEAF PARSLEY

FINE STRIPS OF ZEST FROM A LEMON

2 TABLESPOONS COARSELY CHOPPED PITTED
GREEN OLIVES

SALT AND FRESHLY GROUND BLACK PEPPER

For the lemon dressing

JUICE OF THE ZESTED LEMON USED FOR
THE GREMOLATA

¼ CUP EXTRA VIRGIN OLIVE OIL, PLUS EXTRA
FOR DRIZZLING

1 TEASPOON DIJON MUSTARD

1 TEASPOON HONEY, OR TO TASTE

SALT AND FRESHLY GROUND BLACK PEPPER

Trim the asparagus by snapping off the woody ends, then cut each spear into 2-inch lengths. Bring a saucepan of salted water to a boil and blanch the asparagus for 3 minutes or until tender, then refresh in a bowl of iced water. Not only will this keep the asparagus from cooking any further, but it will also preserve the beautiful, vibrant emerald green color. Blanch the peas in the same pan for 1 to 2 minutes and add to the asparagus. Cook the fava beans in the same water for 1 to 2 minutes and then drain through a colander. Rinse the beans under cold water and then slide each one from its outer jacket to reveal the bright green, tender bean inside. Drain all the veggies and pat dry on paper towels.

To make the gremolata, combine all the ingredients in a small bowl and season with salt and black pepper.

Next make the dressing: Squeeze the juice from the lemon into a bowl, add the olive oil and mustard, and whisk to combine. Taste and add the honey and a seasoning of salt and pepper. Toss the beans, peas, and asparagus in the dressing and arrange on plates with the baby leaf spinach and pea shoots.

Toast the sourdough on both sides under the broiler. Slice the goat cheese into ½-inch thick discs and place one slice on each piece of toast. Flash the cheese under the broiler again until it starts to soften. Spoon the gremolata alongside, drizzle with a little more oil, and serve immediately with the salad.

Thai Pomelo Salad with Lobster and Crab

In Thailand, a variation of this salad minus the seafood is often served alongside curries, but in this instance I've added lobster and crab to make it substantial enough to be served as the hero. If lobster is hard to find or blows your budget, try using freshly cooked shrimp or grilled squid instead.

SERVES 4 AS A LIGHT LUNCH OR PART OF A SHARING TABLE

For the dressing

2 TO 3 BIRD'S EYE CHILES, SEEDED AND FINELY CHOPPED

2 GARLIC CLOVES, FINELY CHOPPED

3 FRESH LIME LEAVES, FINELY SHREDDED

1 LARGE OR 2 SMALL LEMONGRASS STALKS, INNER STALKS TRIMMED AND FINELY SLICED

1 TABLESPOON GRATED FRESH GINGER

¼ CUP LIME JUICE

3 TABLESPOONS PALM OR GRANULATED SUGAR

3 TABLESPOONS FISH SAUCE

3 TABLESPOONS RICE WINE VINEGAR

For the salad

2 POMELOS

1 LARGE COOKED LOBSTER

7 OUNCES FRESHLY COOKED WHITE CRABMEAT

A HANDFUL OF CILANTRO LEAVES

A HANDFUL OF THAI BASIL

FLESH OF ¼ FRESH COCONUT, SHAVED INTO STRIPS USING A VEGETABLE PEELER

3 RED SHALLOTS, FINELY SLICED

Start by making the dressing. Pound the chiles, garlic, lime leaves, and lemongrass together using a mortar and pestle. Add the remaining dressing ingredients and mix until the sugar has dissolved.

Cut a slice off the top and bottom of the pomelos. Stand the pomelos upright on the cutting board and, using a serrated knife and a sawing motion, slice the skin in strips from top to bottom, removing all the pith as you do so. Neatly cut or tear the pomelo into segments by slicing in between the membranes. Gently toss the segments in three-quarters of the dressing and set aside to soak up the flavors while you deal with the shellfish.

Remove the lobster claws and crack the shells with a rolling pin or meat mallet. Carefully remove all the claw meat. Twist the head from the lobster body and reserve for making stock along with all the shell. Using kitchen scissors, cut through the shell on the underside of the lobster body from one end to the other. Carefully pry the shell apart and remove the lobster tail in one piece. Slice the tail meat into thick slices. Pick through the crabmeat and remove any traces of shell.

Arrange the pomelo on plates and top with the lobster and crabmeat. Scatter with the cilantro and basil, and spoon over the remaining dressing. Finish with a flourish of shaved coconut and sliced shallots and serve immediately.

Pomelos are native to Southeast Asia and can be found in most good Thai or specialty Asian grocers, where you can also pick up most of the other ingredients needed to make this salad. Pomelos have a thick, smooth yellowish-green skin and are nearest in looks to a grapefruit, although they can be at least twice the size and often weigh in at over 2¼ pounds, but a large proportion of this is skin and pith.

Tuna Crudo Salad with Pink Grapefruit and Citrus Dressing

Not only does this salad look very pretty, it tastes rather marvelous too. If you prefer, you could use cooked shrimp in place of the tuna and arugula instead of the mizuna. However, if you have a garden or even a small terrace, it's worth growing a few pots of mizuna, as these peppery, sharp salad leaves are about the easiest thing to grow and really add an extra dimension to the salad bowl.

SERVES 4 AS A LIGHT DISH

1 HEAD OF FENNEL

¼ CUP RICE VINEGAR

2 TABLESPOONS GRANULATED SUGAR

A PINCH OF SALT

2 PINK GRAPEFRUITS

9 OUNCES SUSHI-GRADE FRESH TUNA

A HANDUL OF MIZUNA

RED SHISO OR OTHER MICRO HERBS OR SPROUTS

1 TABLESPOON SESAME SEEDS, LIGHTLY TOASTED

NANAMI TOGARSHI (JAPANESE CHILE SEASONING)

For the dressing

2 TABLESPOONS SOY SAUCE

2 TABLESPOONS GRAPEFRUIT, ORANGE, OR MANDARIN JUICE

4 TEASPOONS YUZU OR LIME JUICE

¼ CUP SESAME OIL

FRESHLY GROUND BLACK PEPPER

Start by lightly pickling the fennel: Trim the fennel, cut into quarters, and very finely slice (this is best done using a mandolin if you have one), then transfer to a glass or ceramic bowl. Combine the rice vinegar and sugar in a small saucepan, add the salt, and bring to a boil, swirling the pan to dissolve the sugar. Pour the hot pickling liquid over the fennel and set aside for 30 minutes to soften while you prepare the remaining salad ingredients.

Using a sharp knife, cut a thin slice off the top and bottom of each grapefruit. Sit the grapefruit upright on the cutting board and cut the skin away from the fruit in strips, working from top to bottom, so that you end up with a neat barrel shape with no pith remaining. Neatly cut the grapefruit segments away from the membrane and set aside. Squeeze the juice from the membrane into a bowl—you will need 2 tablespoons for the dressing.

To make the dressing, pour all the ingredients into a small bowl with the grapefruit juice and whisk briefly to combine.

Slice the tuna into neat bite-sized pieces and arrange on plates. Drain the fennel from the pickling liquid and arrange around the tuna with the grapefruit segments. Scatter the mizuna and shiso or other micro herbs or sprouts around, sprinkle with the toasted sesame seeds, drizzle with the dressing, and season with *nanami togarshi*. Serve immediately.

Berries & Soft Fruit

Full of bright sweetness, like a jewel box of colors that marks the start of summer, I don't know anyone who doesn't love a bowl of berries.

The season for berries and soft fruit spans the months from late spring to late summer, starting with almost neon pink hothouse rhubarb in early spring and ending with figs heralding in the fall. With a role call of strawberries, raspberries, gooseberries, currants, blueberries, and blackberries taking their turn to shine in the high summer months, for the cook this is a time of plenty. Although most berries are now available all year round, those that have been imported from the other side of the world months after your local season has finished will be lacking in flavor, sparkle, and sweetness that can only come from fruit picked and eaten in a matter of days.

If you are lucky enough to have your own garden or pick-your-own fruit farm nearby, then you will be aware of how much better soft fruit tastes when picked from the bush at optimum ripeness, still warm from the sunshine and heavy with sweet juice. I remember many afternoons as a child spent at a pick-your-own fruit farm—eating my body weight in juicy strawberries and raspberries and never quite managing to fill a basket, which was the purpose of the exercise.

In my kitchen I prefer to use berries for sweet cooking or preserving rather than in savory food, so in this chapter you'll find recipes for fruit salads, bakes, and desserts where I feel that berries are showcased best. When fruit is this good it only requires simple preparation. I can't think of anything nicer than a bowl of garden-grown strawberries served either with a scoop of vanilla sugar to dip them in, with whipped cream over the top, or with crisp, slightly caramelized brown sugar meringues for crunch and texture.

Figs, however, either fresh or dried, marry well with savory foods and are perfectly matched with tangy cheese, toasted nuts, salty cured ham, and bitter salad leaves. Gooseberries and rhubarb are often paired with rich meats and oily fish such as duck and mackerel, but I like gooseberries best when prepared with something creamy and sweet, such as my recipe for posset on page 71.

Fig, Hazelnut, and Fennel Soda Bread

Soda bread is possibly the easiest bread to make. It requires no rising or messing around with yeast, but does demand a gentle hand and delicate touch to avoid becoming overworked and tough. It's delicious served with good (Irish) butter or with cheese and chutney, and is best eaten on the day of making. I've used soft dried figs here, but you could just as easily use apricots, raisins, or dried cranberries, or walnuts or pecans instead of hazelnuts or almonds.

MAKES 1 LARGE LOAF

2½ CUPS ALL-PURPOSE FLOUR, PLUS EXTRA
FOR DUSTING

1 CUP BLANCHED HAZELNUTS

1 CUP SOFT DRIED FIGS

1½ CUPS WHOLE-GRAIN SPELT OR RYE FLOUR

1 ROUNDED TEASPOON BAKING SODA

1 TEASPOON SEA SALT

1 TEASPOON FENNEL SEEDS

½ TEASPOON FRESHLY GROUND
BLACK PEPPER

2 CUPS BUTTERMILK, PLUS 2 TABLESPOONS

2 TEASPOONS HONEY

A HANDFUL OF SPELT OR RYE FLAKES

Preheat the oven to 350°F. Lightly dust a large baking sheet with flour or cover with parchment paper.

Lightly toast the nuts on a baking sheet in the oven for about 4 minutes or until very pale golden. Very coarsely chop and set aside. Snip off the tough stalk end from each fig and coarsely chop the fruit.

Sift the two flours and baking soda into a large mixing bowl, add the salt, fennel seeds, and black pepper, and mix well. Add the nuts and figs, mix again, then make a well in the middle of the ingredients.

Combine 2 cups buttermilk and honey in a large glass measuring cup, pour into the well, and, using a large spoon or spatula, mix until just combined. Then, using your hands, gently knead the dough—just enough to bring it together. Lightly flour the work surface, lift the dough out, and knead again, keeping it light, as overworking the dough at this stage will result in a leaden loaf. With minimal handling, shape the dough into a round cake shape and transfer to the prepared baking sheet. Brush the top of the loaf with remaining 2 tablespoons of buttermilk. Using a long, sharp knife, score a deep cross in the top and scatter with the spelt or rye flakes. Bake on the middle rack of the oven for about 35 minutes or until golden brown and the loaf sounds hollow when tapped on the bottom. Flip the bread over onto its top and bake for another 3 to 4 minutes, then transfer to a wire rack until cold.

Fig Chutney

I'm giving you two options for a fig relish to serve with cheese or cold cuts here. One uses fresh and the other soft dried figs. I like both equally, but since fresh figs aren't always so easy to find, I often resort to using dried. Neither chutney nor relish are the types that you need to store for months on end before opening to allow the vinegar to mellow—they can be eaten pretty much right away.

Fresh

MAKES 2 JARS

8 LARGE FRESH FIGS

1 ONION OR 2 LARGE SHALLOTS, FINELY CHOPPED

2-INCH PIECE OF FRESH GINGER, FINELY GRATED

1 CUP LIGHT BROWN SUGAR

⅔ CUP CIDER VINEGAR

2 TEASPOONS YELLOW MUSTARD SEEDS

1 CINNAMON STICK

1 BAY LEAF

A PINCH OF ALLSPICE

SALT AND FRESHLY GROUND BLACK PEPPER

Equipment
2 × 16-OUNCE CANNING JARS

Trim the tough stalk from each fig, coarsely chop the fruit, and put in a large, stainless steel saucepan. Add all the remaining ingredients and season well. Place the pan over low to medium heat and stir frequently until the sugar has dissolved.

Bring to a boil and then, keeping the heat at a gentle simmer, cook for about 30 minutes, stirring frequently to prevent the chutney from scorching on the bottom of the pan, until it has turned into a tender, glossy, sticky relish.

Remove the cinnamon stick and bay leaf, spoon into sterilized canning jars (see page 132), leaving ¼ to ½ inch headspace, seal with lids, and process in a water bath (see page 40). Let cool, label, and store in a cool, dark cupboard for up to 6 months. Store in the fridge once opened for up to 1 month.

Dried

MAKES 2 JARS

1 CUP SOFT DRIED FIGS, COARSELY CHOPPED

⅓ CUP RAISINS, GOLDEN RAISINS, OR CHOPPED SOFT DRIED DATES

1 LARGE SHALLOT, SLICED

1 SMALL SWEET APPLE, PEELED AND DICED

½ CUP LIGHT BROWN SUGAR

½ CUP CIDER VINEGAR

1 TEASPOON FINELY GRATED ORANGE ZEST

1 CINNAMON STICK

1 BAY LEAF

SALT AND FRESHLY GROUND BLACK PEPPER

Equipment
2 × 16-OUNCE CANNING JARS

Put the figs in a large, stainless steel saucepan. Add the raisins, golden raisins, or chopped dates—whichever you prefer—along with all the remaining ingredients, except the seasoning. Place the pan over low to medium heat and stir frequently until the sugar has dissolved.

Bring to a boil, then reduce to a simmer and cook for about 25 minutes, stirring frequently, until thickened, glossy, and jam-like.

Remove the cinnamon stick and bay leaf, season with salt and black pepper, and let cool, then spoon into sterilized canning jars (see page 132), leaving ¼ to ½ inch headspace, seal with lids, and process in a water bath (see page 40). Store in the fridge for 2 months.

Fig and Goat Cheese Tart

This little tart is just perfect to serve for a light lunch—not only does it look pretty but it takes no time at all to prepare and is super tasty to boot. All it needs is a salad of some peppery leaves such as arugula and mizuna, a drizzle of balsamic vinegar dressing, and a light scattering of Parmesan shavings.

SERVES 4

ALL-PURPOSE FLOUR, FOR DUSTING

9 OUNCES ALL-BUTTER PUFF PASTRY

2 MEDIUM EGGS

1 MEDIUM EGG YOLK

⅔ CUP HEAVY CREAM

SALT AND FRESHLY GROUND BLACK PEPPER

4 TO 6 FRESH FIGS

3½ OUNCES GORGONZOLA OR
SOFT GOAT CHEESE

2 TABLESPOONS PINE NUTS

2 SPRIGS OF THYME, LEAVES PICKED

AGED BALSAMIC VINEGAR AND EXTRA VIRGIN
OLIVE OIL, FOR DRIZZLING

Equipment

4 × 14-INCH TART PAN

Lightly dust the work surface with flour and roll the pastry out into a rectangle 1 inch bigger than the tart pan on all sides. Carefully lift the pastry into the pan—being careful not to stretch the dough—and press it into the corners, lining the bottom and sides evenly. Pop into the freezer for 30 minutes while you preheat the oven to 400°F and place a solid baking sheet on the middle rack to heat up.

Prepare the filling. In a bowl, beat the whole eggs and egg yolk with the cream until thoroughly combined and season well with salt and black pepper. Trim the tough stalk from each fig and cut each fig in half. Prick the bottom of the tart crust with a fork and pour in the egg mixture. Crumble the cheese on top and arrange the fig halves evenly between the cheese, cut-side up. Scatter with the pine nuts and thyme leaves.

Carefully slide the tart onto the hot baking sheet and bake for 15 minutes until the filling has started to set and the crust starts to turn crisp and golden. Reduce the heat to 350°F and cook for another 15 minutes.

Remove from the oven and let cool slightly before serving drizzled with aged balsamic vinegar and extra virgin olive oil.

Fig and Blue Cheese Salad

This is barely a recipe—more of a serving suggestion, but a mighty fine one at that. A stroll around a French or Italian market in early autumn will provide all the ingredients necessary for this salad. Perfectly ripe figs, tangy, grassy blue cheese such as a goat's milk Persillé du Marais, Cote Hill Blue, Roquefort, Gorgonzola, or Regalis and slices of Ibérico, Bayonne, Serrano, or Prosciutto. Packaged in waxed paper and eaten while admiring the view in a picturesque spot somewhere… the best things are often the simplest.

SERVES 3 TO 4

2 HEADS OF CHICORY

1 HEAD OF RADICCHIO OR TREVISO TARDIVE

7 OUNCES BLUE CHEESE (SEE RECIPE INTRODUCTION)

A GOOD HANDFUL OF CHOPPED TOASTED HAZELNUTS

6 RIPE FIGS

8 SLICES OF CURED HAM (SEE RECIPE INTRODUCTION)

A GENEROUS DRIZZLE OF FRUITY EXTRA VIRGIN OLIVE OIL

A NOT-SO-GENEROUS DRIZZLE OF AGED BALSAMIC VINEGAR

SALT AND FRESHLY GROUND BLACK PEPPER

SOURDOUGH BREAD, TO SERVE

Wash the salad leaves in cold water and dry on a clean kitchen towel, then arrange on a plate. Crumble over the cheese and scatter with the hazelnuts. Cut or tear the figs into quarters or bite-sized pieces and arrange over the leaves with the slices of ham.

Drizzle with the olive oil and balsamic vinegar, season with salt and black pepper, and serve with some crusty sourdough bread to mop up the dressing.

Gooseberry Gelatin Dessert

If making this at the start of the gooseberry season when elderflowers are still in bloom, pick a handful of flower heads and add to the fruit as it cooks to add a fragrant, floral note. As always when using fresh flowers in cooking, ensure that they are washed, not picked from the roadside, bug free, and unsprayed with chemicals. Add a dash of elderflower cordial if you prefer, but go easy, as you don't want to overpower the delicate gooseberry flavor.

Sheet gelatin has a milder flavor than powdered and is available in different setting strengths—I always use platinum grade, which gives a stronger set for fewer sheets, and is available in most supermarkets or online. I have given two quantities here: use the lesser one if you plan to serve the gelatin in pretty glasses with a slightly softer set and the higher quantity for a firmer, wobbly gelatin set into a mold and turned onto a plate. If planning on the latter, I'd recommend that you make it at least 24 and up to 48 hours before serving—it will hold its shape better the longer you let it set.

MAKES 1 LARGE GELATIN OR
6 TO 8 GLASSES

2¾ POUNDS GOOSEBERRIES, RINSED (NO
NEED TO TRIM)

⅔ TO ¾ CUP GRANULATED SUGAR, TO TASTE

7 TO 9 SHEETS OF PLATINUM-GRADE LEAF
GELATIN (SEE RECIPE INTRODUCTION)

SUNFLOWER OIL, FOR OILING (IF USING
A MOLD)

WHITECURRANTS OR ELDERFLOWERS,
TO DECORATE

LIGHT CREAM, TO SERVE

Equipment

JELLY STRAINER BAG

1-QUART JELLY MOLD (OPTIONAL)

If you are partial to the odd cocktail, do as I do and, once you've strained off all the gooseberry juice, pour the fruit pulp into a preserving jar, add a handful of elderflowers, and pour in a bottle of gin. Seal tightly, give the jar a shake, and leave in the fridge for 1 month, shaking every other day or when you remember. Strain through cheesecloth and use as you see fit—it's good as a Martini and gives a G&T an unusual twist.

Put the gooseberries in a large saucepan with 2 cups cold water. Set over low to medium heat, half cover, and bring slowly to a boil. Reduce the heat to a gentle simmer and cook until the berries have burst, stirring with a wooden spoon to break up the fruit.

Pour into a jelly strainer bag suspended over a large bowl. Allow the juice to slowly drip into the bowl but do not squeeze the bag or prod the fruit—leave the juice to drip through until the skin and seeds are all that's left in the bag, which can take a good few hours. Measure the resulting juice—you should have about 1 quart—add the sugar to taste, and stir well to dissolve.

Soak the gelatin sheets in a large bowl of cold water for 10 minutes to soften. Pour half the gooseberry juice into a pan, heat to just boiling, and then remove from the heat. Drain the gelatin sheets, squeeze out any excess water, and blot quickly on a clean kitchen towel or paper towels, then add to the hot juice. Stir well until completely melted, add the reserved juice, stirring to combine, and let cool to room temperature. Pour into glasses or a very lightly oiled jelly mold, then place on a baking sheet, slide into the fridge, and leave until set. This will take at least 24 hours for glasses and longer—see introduction—for molds.

Quickly dip the jelly mold, if using, in a bowl of just-boiled water to loosen the sides and carefully turn onto a serving plate. Serve the dessert decorated with whitecurrants or elderflowers, with a little cold light cream.

Gooseberry Posset with Gingery Thins

Most people are more familiar with posset (a British dessert similar to syllabub) made from lemons. In this twist, I've stuck with the usual three ingredients but used cooked gooseberries in place of the lemons, which are often folded into whipped cream to make a fool—something I love for its simplicity and the fact that it's somewhat old-fashioned. The result is an altogether more sophisticated dessert, although no harder to make. As posset is quite rich, I like to serve it in small, elegant glasses with something crisp on the side, so while the posset is chilling, use your time wisely and rustle up these Gingery Thins.

SERVES 4 TO 6; MAKES ABOUT
30 THINS

For the posset

14 OUNCES GOOSEBERRIES,
RINSED AND TRIMMED

⅔ CUP GRANULATED SUGAR

2 CUPS HEAVY CREAM

For the gingery thins

9 TABLESPOONS UNSALTED BUTTER,
SOFTENED

¼ CUP LIGHT BROWN SUGAR

1 TABLESPOON CORN SYRUP

1¼ CUPS ALL-PURPOSE FLOUR, PLUS EXTRA
FOR DUSTING

¼ CUP GROUND ALMONDS

¼ TEASPOON BAKING POWDER

¼ TEASPOON BAKING SODA

1 TEASPOON GROUND GINGER

½ TEASPOON GROUND CINNAMON

A GRATING OF NUTMEG

A PINCH OF SALT

3 TO 4 NUGGETS OF CANDIED GINGER
(OPTIONAL)

Equipment

FINE-MESH NYLON SIEVE

2½-INCH FLUTED COOKIE CUTTER

Start by making the posset. Put the gooseberries in a saucepan, add 2 tablespoons of cold water, cover, and cook over low to medium heat for about 15 minutes until the fruit has become really soft and juicy. Pour into a fine-mesh nylon sieve set over a bowl and let the juice drip through for about 40 minutes.

Measure the juice—you should have around ¾ cup—and pour back into the clean pan. Bring to a boil and reduce over medium heat until you have ½ cup remaining. Remove from the heat, add the sugar, and stir until dissolved.

Pour the cream into a separate clean saucepan and bring to a boil. Immediately remove the pan from the heat, pour the cream over the gooseberry syrup, and whisk until silky smooth. Pour the posset into delicate glasses and leave until cold before covering with plastic wrap and popping in the fridge for about 4 hours to set.

Meanwhile, make the thins. Cream the butter and sugar in a bowl until pale and fluffy. Mix in the corn syrup. Sift in the dry ingredients and, using a rubber spatula or wooden spoon, mix until the dough comes together into a smooth ball. Flatten into a disc, cover with plastic wrap, and chill for about 1 hour until firm.

Preheat the oven to 350°F. Lightly dust the work surface with flour and roll out the dough to a thickness of 1⁄16-inch. Using a 2½-inch cutter, stamp out rounds and arrange on parchment paper–lined baking sheets. Re-roll the scraps and stamp out more cookies. Garnish with a piece of ginger on top of each thin, if using.

Bake one pan at a time on the middle rack of the oven for 9 to 10 minutes until the this are crisp. Cool slightly on the baking sheets and then transfer to a wire rack until cold.

Gooseberry Meringue Tarts

This nutty tart crust doesn't require overly delicate handling or messing around with a rolling pin, and is therefore ideal for pastry phobes. Gooseberry curd also makes a wonderful filling for a simple Victoria cake or roulade.

MAKES 8 TO 12

For the dough

¾ CUP BLANCHED HAZELNUTS, TOASTED

9 TABLESPOONS UNSALTED BUTTER, CHILLED AND DICED

1⅓ CUPS ALL-PURPOSE FLOUR

¼ CUP CONFECTIONERS' SUGAR

A PINCH OF SALT

1 LARGE EGG YOLK (KEEP THE WHITE FOR THE MERINGUE)

For the gooseberry curd

1 POUND GOOSEBERRIES, WASHED

⅔ CUP GRANULATED SUGAR, OR TO TASTE

3 TABLESPOONS UNSALTED BUTTER, DICED

2 LARGE EGGS

1 LARGE EGG YOLK (KEEP THE WHITE FOR THE MERINGUE)

For the meringue

2 LARGE EGG WHITES—USE ONE FROM THE DOUGH AND ONE FROM THE CURD

A PINCH OF SALT

½ CUP GRANULATED SUGAR

Equipment

8 TO 12 INDIVIDUAL TART PANS

FINE-MESH NYLON SIEVE

LARGE PIPING BAG FITTED WITH A LARGE STAR NOZZLE

Start by making the dough: Process the hazelnuts in a food processor until finely chopped. Add the butter, flour, confectioners' sugar, and salt and pulse until the mixture resembles bread crumbs. Add the egg yolk, blend briefly—just enough to bring the dough together—then turn onto the work surface and gather it together with your hands, although try not to knead it. Shape into a ball, cover with plastic wrap, and chill for 30 minutes.

Break off a walnut-sized nugget of dough and press it into one of the tart pans, covering the bottom and sides evenly and pinching off any excess from the top. Repeat with the remaining pans. Prick the bottoms with a fork and chill for 20 minutes while you preheat the oven to 350°F.

Bake the tart crusts on a baking sheet on the middle rack for about 12 to 15 minutes until golden and crisp. Let cool in the pans. Reduce the oven temperature to 325°F.

Meanwhile, make the curd: Pour the gooseberries into a pan with 2 tablespoons of cold water, cover, and cook over low to medium heat, stirring occasionally, for about 15 minutes, until very mushy. Push through a fine-mesh nylon sieve into a clean saucepan and cook over low heat until the purée thickens to a soft jam consistency. Add the sugar and butter and stir until the butter has melted and the sugar dissolved. Whisk together the whole eggs and yolk and add to the pan, stirring constantly. Cook until the mixture thickens enough to coat the back of a spoon, being careful not to allow it to boil. Taste and add more sugar if necessary. Strain into a clean bowl, cover the surface with plastic wrap to prevent a skin from forming, and let cool. Spoon the cold curd into the tart crusts, filling them to within 1/16-inch of the top and spreading evenly with the back of the spoon.

To make the meringue, pour the egg whites into a large, spotlessly clean mixing bowl, add the salt, then whisk until the egg whites will hold a stiff peak. Gradually add the sugar, a tablespoon at a time, whisking well after each addition, until the meringue is very stiff and glossy.

Scoop into the piping bag and pipe generous swirls on top of the gooseberry curd. Bake for 10 minutes until the meringue is tinged golden brown at the edges. Serve at room temperature.

Rhubarb and Almond Tart

I love this tart with its contrast of sharp yet sweet vanilla and rose-scented rhubarb, nutty frangipane, and flaky, buttery pastry crust. As a bonus, you don't need any fancy pans and it can be put together in no time at all. The rhubarb is very lightly softened in syrup before being baked on top of the tart. If you aren't keen on rosewater, simply leave it out, and the frangipane would work equally well with a mixture of half almonds and half pistachios. Whichever way you bake this tart, be sure to serve it with plenty of cold crème fraîche or a big scoop of vanilla ice cream.

SERVES 6

14 OUNCES SLIM-STEMMED RHUBARB

1 CUP GRANULATED SUGAR

1 TO 2 TEASPOONS ROSEWATER

½ VANILLA BEAN, SPLIT IN HALF LENGTHWISE, OR 1 TEASPOON VANILLA BEAN PASTE

ALL-PURPOSE FLOUR, FOR DUSTING

1 × 14-OUNCE PACKAGE STORE-BOUGHT ALL-BUTTER PUFF PASTRY

2 TABLESPOONS MILK

1 MEDIUM EGG YOLK, LIGHTLY BEATEN

1 ROUNDED TABLESPOON SLICED ALMONDS

For the frangipane

⅔ CUP GROUND ALMONDS

3 TABLESPOONS UNSALTED BUTTER, SOFTENED

¼ CUP GRANULATED SUGAR

1 MEDIUM EGG

1 TEASPOON VANILLA EXTRACT

1 TEASPOON FINELY GRATED LEMON ZEST

A PINCH OF SALT

Rinse the rhubarb under cold running water and trim the ends. Cut each stem into lengths of about 2 inches. Put the sugar, rosewater, and vanilla in a sauté pan and add ¾ cup cold water. Bring slowly to a boil to dissolve the sugar and then remove from the heat. Add the rhubarb, cover, and let soften in the hot syrup.

Lightly dust the work surface with flour and roll out the pastry into a rough oval or round shape—I don't think you need worry too much about neatness for this tart so long as the pastry is about 1⁄16-inch thick and the shape about 14 × 9 inches. Use a large knife to trim and neaten the edges. Carefully slide the pastry onto a large parchment-lined baking sheet, brush the milk around the edges of the pastry, and crimp and fold over to create a border. Chill in the fridge for 20 minutes.

Meanwhile, preheat the oven to 400°F and make the frangipane. Put all the ingredients in a mixing bowl and beat well until smooth.

Spread the frangipane over the pastry, leaving a ½-inch border all the way around as it will spread slightly during cooking. Drain the cooled rhubarb from the syrup and scatter with the frangipane. Brush the edges of the pastry with the beaten egg yolk and scatter the tart with the sliced almonds. Bake on the middle rack of the oven for 10 minutes and then reduce the temperature to 350°F and cook for another 20 to 25 minutes until the frangipane is golden, the pastry crust crisp, and the rhubarb tender. Best served warm, with a light dusting of confectioners' sugar, on the day of making.

Rhubarb and Raspberry Cordial

Homemade cordials are way more delicious and vastly superior to store-bought versions, which can be loaded with preservatives and colors and often barely relate to the fruit from which they are supposedly derived. They're an ideal way to make the most of the season's best produce or to use up a glut. Their shelf life is not long, but if you have space, try freezing the undiluted cordial in ice cube trays and when ready to use, dilute with still or sparkling water to taste. I've kept the base recipe simple, but you can add a couple of slices of fresh ginger to the fruit as it cooks, or rose petals—fresh (unsprayed) or dried—vanilla, sliced strawberries, or even fresh herbs such as mint or basil.

MAKES ABOUT 24 OUNCES

2¼ POUNDS TRIMMED PINK OR SCARLET RHUBARB, WASHED AND CUT INTO 1 TO 1½-INCH LENGTHS

7 OUNCES RASPBERRIES

1¼ CUPS SUGAR

JUICE OF ½ LEMON

SODA WATER OR LEMONADE, FOR DILUTING

ICE, TO SERVE

Equipment

JELLY STRAINER BAG OR LARGE PIECE OF CLEAN CHEESECLOTH

24-OUNCE JAR OR BOTTLE

Place the rhubarb in a large saucepan with the raspberries. Add 2 cups cold water and bring to a gentle simmer. Half cover the pan and cook the fruit very gently for about 25 minutes until it is very tender and has released lots of lovely pink juice. Remove from the heat and let cool for about 2 hours—after which time the juice will have increased in color quite significantly.

Pour the contents of the pan through a jelly strainer bag (or large piece of clean cheesecloth draped over a fine-mesh sieve) into a clean saucepan—don't be tempted to push and press the pulp, otherwise you'll end up with purée rather than a sparkling clear, bright pink juice. It can take at least an hour for all the juice to strain through, so be patient.

Add the sugar and half the lemon juice and bring slowly to a boil to dissolve the sugar, then simmer gently for 5 minutes. Remove from the heat and let cool, then taste and add a dash more lemon juice if needed. Pour into a sterilized jar or bottle (see page 132) and keep refrigerated until ready to use.

Serve over ice diluted with soda water or lemonade, or as a dashing pink gin fizz cocktail—see the recipe below.

Gin and Rhubarb Fizz

SERVES 1

2 PARTS GIN

3 PARTS RHUBARB AND RASPBERRY CORDIAL

DASH OF LEMON JUICE

1 TEASPOON LIGHTLY BEATEN EGG WHITE

ICE CUBES AND TONIC WATER, TO SERVE

RASPBERRIES, TO DECORATE

Place the gin and cordial with the lemon juice and egg white in a cocktail shaker and shake really well.

Half fill a tall glass with ice cubes and tonic water and pour in the pink gin mixture. Decorate with raspberries and perhaps a mint sprig if you're feeling extra fancy.

Strawberry and Rhubarb Compote with Brown Sugar Meringues

Strawberries and rhubarb are a winning combination, one fruit balancing the other for sweet and sour, and the color of the two fruits together is eye popping. This might seem like a curious way to make meringues, but I find it foolproof. They remain in beautiful peaky mounds rather than spreading during cooking and have crisp, shiny shells and marshmallow centers. Using brown sugar adds a toffee-like note.

SERVES 8

For the meringues

¾ CUP GRANULATED SUGAR

⅔ CUP EGG WHITES (3 TO 4 LARGE)

A PINCH OF SALT

1 TEASPOON VANILLA BEAN PASTE

½ CUP LIGHT BROWN SUGAR

⅓ CUP WHOLE BLANCHED HAZELNUTS, COARSELY CHOPPED

For the compote

¼ CUP GRANULATED SUGAR

3 STRIPS OF ORANGE PEEL

½ VANILLA BEAN, SPLIT IN HALF LENGTHWISE

1 POUND STEMMED RHUBARB, WASHED, TRIMMED, AND CUT INTO 1 TO 1½-INCH LENGTHS

1 POUND STRAWBERRIES, HULLED AND HALVED OR QUARTERED

1¼ CUPS HEAVY CREAM

To make the meringues, preheat the oven to 375°F. Heat the sugar in a roasting pan on the middle rack for 5 minutes until hot to the touch. Meanwhile, pour the egg whites into the bowl of a free-standing mixer fitted with the whisk attachment and add the salt. Once the sugar is hot, turn the oven down to 225°F and whisk the egg whites until they will almost hold a stiff peak.

Quickly add the hot sugar to the egg whites in one go, add the vanilla, and whisk on a fast speed for 3 minutes until the meringue has become stiff and glossy and the sugar has dissolved. Gradually add the brown sugar, a tablespoon at a time, whisking constantly until it has been thoroughly incorporated and the meringue has cooled. It should be silky smooth without any grains of sugar. If the sugar hasn't completely dissolved, whisk for another minute or so.

Using a large spoon and palette knife, shape the meringue into 8 mounds on a large parchment paper-lined baking sheet. Scatter with the hazelnuts. Bake on the middle rack of the oven for 1¾ hours until crisp. Turn the oven off and leave the meringues inside to cool down for another 45 minutes.

For the compote, place the sugar, orange peel, and vanilla bean in a sauté pan and add ½ cup water. Bring slowly to a boil to dissolve the sugar, then add the rhubarb, cover, and leave over a gentle heat for 2 to 3 minutes to soften. Test the rhubarb for doneness with the tip of a sharp knife—you want it to be tender but still to hold its shape. If it's still a little firm, cook for another minute or so. Remove from the heat, add the strawberries, and stir in gently. Let cool.

Whip the cream until it holds soft luscious peaks—I always do this by hand rather than using a hand-held mixer, as it reduces the risk of over-whipping. Place one meringue on each plate and pile with a good dollop of whipped cream, then top with a generous spoonful of the compote and a good drizzle of syrup. Eat immediately.

Roasted Strawberry Ice Cream

I've said it many times, but the success of all fruit recipes lies in using ripe, seasonal produce. And this is most certainly the case with strawberries. The best strawberries I have ever eaten come from a small family-run farm in Warwickshire, England. The berries are sold direct from the farm shop and their season lasts only a couple of weeks—blink and you'll miss them. It would be almost criminal to do anything to them other than to pull out the stems and eat them *au naturel*, straight from the container.

I'm not normally a fan of cooking with strawberries (unless in jam making), so I'm bending my own rules in this recipe. But roasting the strawberries here really intensifies the flavor, slightly caramelizing the sugar and giving a jamminess to the fruit and a boost to the ice cream. If you're not able to make it to a certain farm in Warwickshire, this is an ideal way to use up less-than-perfect fruit.

SERVES 6

2¼ POUNDS STRAWBERRIES, HULLED

1 CUP GRANULATED SUGAR

1 VANILLA BEAN, SPLIT IN HALF LENGTHWISE

2 STRIPS OF PEEL FROM A LEMON

1½ CUPS HEAVY CREAM

½ CUP WHOLE MILK

4 MEDIUM EGG YOLKS

Equipment

FINE-MESH NYLON SIEVE

ICE-CREAM MAKER

PLASTIC FREEZER-SAFE CONTAINER

Preheat the oven to 350°F. Put the strawberries in an ovenproof ceramic dish or a baking pan lined with parchment paper. Toss with ¼ cup of the sugar and tuck one half of the vanilla bean and the lemon peels in with the berries. Cook on the middle rack of the oven for about 40 minutes until slumped and juicy. Discard the vanilla bean half and the peel, and transfer the strawberries and all of their juice into the bowl of a food processor and blend until smooth.

Heat the cream and milk with the remaining vanilla bean half in a saucepan over medium heat until just below boiling point. Meanwhile, using a hand-held mixer, beat together the remaining ¾ cup of sugar and the egg yolks in a bowl until very pale and thick. Add the hot cream mixture in a steady stream, beating constantly until smooth. Return to the pan and cook over low heat, stirring constantly with a wooden spoon, until it thickens enough to coat the back of the spoon, but don't allow it to boil, otherwise the eggs may scramble. Strain through a fine-mesh nylon sieve into a clean bowl and let cool completely, then thoroughly chill in the fridge for at least 2 hours but preferably overnight.

Whisk three-quarters of the strawberry purée into the custard and churn in an ice-cream maker according to the manufacturer's instructions. Scoop the ice cream into a plastic freezer-safe container and very lightly stir through the remaining strawberry purée—it should still be visible in ripples. Cover and freeze until firm.

Sunken Chocolate and Raspberry Cake

This cake is more suited as a dessert rather than an afternoon cake. It is almost a baked mousse and it will crack and sink as it cools—which is part of its charm—beauty in imperfection if you like. Serve with a generous dusting of confectioners' sugar, a mound of fresh raspberries, and some vanilla ice cream.

SERVES 8 TO 10

17 TABLESPOONS (2 STICKS PLUS 1 TABLESPOON) UNSALTED BUTTER, CUT INTO PIECES, PLUS EXTRA FOR GREASING

⅓ CUP ALL-PURPOSE FLOUR, PLUS EXTRA FOR DUSTING

9 OUNCES DARK CHOCOLATE, 70% COCOA SOLIDS, BROKEN INTO PIECES

6 LARGE EGGS, SEPARATED

1 TEASPOON VANILLA EXTRACT

1 CUP GRANULATED SUGAR

⅓ CUP LIGHT BROWN SUGAR

A PINCH OF SALT

½ CUP GROUND ALMONDS

5 OUNCES RASPBERRIES, PLUS EXTRA TO SERVE

CONFECTIONERS' SUGAR, FOR DUSTING

Equipment

9-INCH SPRINGFORM CAKE PAN

Preheat the oven to 350°F. Grease and line the bottom of the cake pan with greased parchment paper. Lightly dust the pan with flour, tapping out the excess.

Melt the chocolate with the butter in a heatproof bowl, either in the microwave on a low setting or over a saucepan of barely simmering water. Stir until smooth and let cool slightly.

Using a free-standing mixer fitted with the whisk attachment, whisk the egg yolks, vanilla extract, and granulated and brown sugars together until thick and pale, doubled in volume, and the mixture leaves a ribbon trail when the whisk is lifted from the bowl, scraping down the sides of the bowl once or twice.

In a separate bowl, whisk the egg whites with the salt until they hold stiff but not dry peaks. Using a large metal spoon, fold the melted chocolate and butter into the egg yolk mixture. Sift the ground almonds and flour into the bowl and fold in along with the raspberries. Fold one-third of the egg whites into the mixture to loosen it and then fold in the remainder, being careful not to knock out the air.

Spoon the mixture into the prepared pan and bake on the middle rack of the oven for 25 to 30 minutes until the cake is starting to crack around the edges and the middle is set. Remove from the oven and let the cake cool in the pan—it will sink and crack as it cools.

Carefully run a palette knife around the edges of the pan to loosen the cake, remove from the pan, and place on a serving plate. Scatter with extra raspberries and dust with confectioners' sugar to serve.

Pickled Redcurrants

Serve these jeweled, pickled redcurrants alongside hearty pâtés and cold cuts.

MAKES 2 JARS

1½ CUPS WHITE WINE VINEGAR

¼ CUP GRANULATED SUGAR

3 ALLSPICE BERRIES

2 CLOVES

1 BAY LEAF

11 OUNCES REDCURRANTS

Equipment

2 × 16-OUNCE CANNING JARS

Bring the vinegar to a boil in a small stainless steel saucepan with the sugar, allspice, and cloves. Add the bay leaf and simmer for 5 minutes, then remove from the heat and let cool.

Meanwhile, wash the redcurrants in cold running water and let dry either on a clean kitchen towel or paper towels.

Pack the fruit into two sterilized jars (see page 132) and pour in the cooled vinegar, leaving ¼ to ½ inch headspace. Seal the jars and process in a water bath (see page 40). Leave in a cool, dark place for about 4 weeks before serving. They will keep for about 3 months in a cool, dark cupboard. Once opened, store in the fridge for up to 3 months.

Lemon and Almond Roulade with Redcurrants and Raspberries

Just occasionally I do like a show-offy type of dessert, and when I do, a roulade fits the bill nicely. The almonds, both ground and sliced, give this cake a delicate flavor, sophisticated air, and lightness, while the sharpness of the redcurrants cuts through the richness of the cream. And crisp, sugar-frosted strands of redcurrants—although somewhat retro—complete the picture. Although I've often served this roulade as a dessert on a summer's day, it wouldn't be out of place at a fancy afternoon party.

SERVES 6 TO 8

2 TABLESPOONS UNSALTED BUTTER, MELTED AND SLIGHTLY COOLED, PLUS EXTRA, MELTED, FOR GREASING

⅔ CUP ALL-PURPOSE FLOUR, PLUS EXTRA FOR DUSTING

5 MEDIUM EGGS

⅔ CUP GRANULATED SUGAR, PLUS 3 TABLESPOONS

FINELY GRATED ZEST OF ½ LEMON

1 TEASPOON BAKING POWDER

¾ CUP GROUND ALMONDS

A PINCH OF SALT

½ CUP SLICED ALMONDS

For the filling

9 OUNCES REDCURRANTS

1 TABLESPOON GRANULATED SUGAR

1¼ CUPS HEAVY CREAM

5 OUNCES RASPBERRIES, PLUS EXTRA TO DECORATE

CONFECTIONERS' SUGAR, FOR DUSTING

For the frosted redcurrants

7 OUNCES REDCURRANTS, IN CLUSTERS

1 MEDIUM EGG WHITE, LIGHTLY BEATEN WITH 1 TEASPOON COLD WATER

¾ CUP GRANULATED SUGAR

Equipment

12 × 15-INCH SWISS ROLL PAN

Preheat the oven to 350°F. Grease the pan with melted butter and line the bottom and sides with a large sheet of parchment paper. Grease the parchment and lightly dust with flour, tapping out the excess.

Using a free-standing mixer fitted with the whisk attachment, whisk the eggs and the ⅔ cup of granulated sugar until very thick and pale, tripled in volume, and the mixture leaves a ribbon trail when the whisk is lifted from the bowl. Add the lemon zest and sift in all the dry ingredients, except the sliced almonds, then, using a large metal spoon and a figure-eight action, gently fold in. Pour the melted butter around the edges of the bowl and fold in.

Gently pour into the prepared pan, spread level, and scatter with the sliced almonds. Bake on the middle rack of the oven for about 12 minutes until golden and just firm to the touch. Meanwhile, lay a large sheet of parchment paper on the work surface and sprinkle it with the remaining 3 tablespoons of granulated sugar.

Let the baked cake rest for a minute before turning onto the sugared parchment—this takes a leap of faith, but you simply hold the pan at both ends and flip it out in one quick movement. Carefully peel off the lining paper and then roll up the cake, starting from the shortest end and with the clean parchment rolled inside the cake. Let cool completely.

For the filling, strip the redcurrants from the stalks, place in a saucepan with the sugar, and cook over medium heat until they have burst. Continue to cook, stirring frequently, until thickened to a purée with the consistency of a soft-set jam. Remove from the heat and cool.

For the frosted redcurrants, using a small clean brush, paint the redcurrant clusters with the egg white solution

and then sprinkle evenly and thickly with the sugar. Let dry on a wire rack.

Whip the cream into soft, pillowy peaks. Unroll the cake and spread the surface evenly with the redcurrant purée. Using a palette knife, spread the cream on top, leaving a ½-inch border all around the edge. Scatter with the raspberries, lightly crushing them in your fingers as you do so. Re-roll the roulade as tightly as possible, using the parchment to help you lift and roll. Carefully slide onto a serving plate, dust with confectioners' sugar, and decorate with the frosted redcurrants and extra raspberries.

Peach and Blackcurrant Pie

My mother makes a stunning peach and blackcurrant compote that she often serves with her famous meringues and a pitcher of cold cream. It will forever remind me of lazy summer lunches in her colorful garden sitting under a large parasol. She also makes a mean fruit pie, so I've combined the two here to make what I think is something rather special. If you can't get hold of fresh blackcurrants, you could use blueberries at a pinch, but they won't have the tartness of blackcurrants, so go easy on the sugar. Serve this pie warm with cold cream or scoops of vanilla ice cream.

SERVES 8

For the dough

2½ CUPS ALL-PURPOSE FLOUR, PLUS EXTRA FOR DUSTING

A GOOD PINCH OF SEA SALT

13 TABLESPOONS UNSALTED BUTTER, DICED AND CHILLED

¼ CUP GRANULATED SUGAR, PLUS EXTRA FOR SPRINKLING

3 TABLESPOONS ICED WATER

2 TEASPOONS CIDER VINEGAR OR LEMON JUICE

½ MEDIUM EGG WHITE, LIGHTLY BEATEN

For the filling

4 LARGE RIPE PEACHES, WASHED AND EACH CUT INTO 6 WEDGES

7 OUNCES BLACKCURRANTS

2 TO 3 TABLESPOONS GRANULATED SUGAR

FINELY GRATED ZEST OF ½ LEMON

1 ROUNDED TABLESPOON CORNSTARCH

1 TABLESPOON UNSALTED BUTTER

Equipment

8 TO 9-INCH DEEP PIE DISH OR OVENPROOF SKILLET

Start by making the dough. Put the flour in a large mixing bowl, add the salt and butter, and, using a round-bladed knife, cut the butter into the flour so that it starts to be rubbed in. Use your fingers to continue rubbing the butter into the flour, lifting the mixture up out of the bowl and letting it almost roll over your fingertips. Be careful not to overwork—the butter should be incorporated into the flour with a few flecks still visible. Mix in the sugar with the knife.

Combine the iced water and vinegar or lemon juice in a cup and add two-thirds to the bowl. Mix in with the knife until the dough starts to come together, adding more if necessary. Gather the dough together, trying not to knead it, and shape into a ball. Flatten into a disc, cover with plastic wrap, and chill for a good 2 hours.

Cut off one-third of the dough, cover, and refrigerate until needed. Roll out the larger piece on a lightly floured work surface into a disc 11 to 12 inches in diameter. Carefully roll it around the rolling pin and then unroll into the pie dish so that it covers the bottom and sides evenly, with a little excess draped over the sides. Without stretching the dough, press it into the corners. Using a sharp knife, trim off any excess, gather into a ball, and save for the lattice. Chill for 20 minutes while you prepare the filling and preheat the oven to 350°F. Place a baking sheet on the middle rack while the oven heats up.

Gently mix all the filling ingredients, except the butter, in a bowl without breaking up the fruit. Spoon into the pie crust and dot the filling with butter.

Dust the work surface with a little flour and roll out half the reserved dough into a disc slightly larger than the top of the pie. Cut into 12 × ½-inch wide strips and arrange in a lattice over the fruit. Trim off any excess dough, gather into a ball with the offcuts, and roll out to a strip 2 inches wide and about 20 inches long. Cut into 3 × ½-inch wide strips and carefully plait together. Brush the top edge of the pie with water and lay the plait around it. Brush all the dough with the beaten egg white, sprinkle with granulated sugar, and bake on the hot baking sheet for 40 to 45 minutes until the filling is bubbling and the crust golden brown and crisp. Serve at room temperature.

Blueberry and Lemon Verbena Buttermilk Sherbet

Blueberries and buttermilk are combined to make this light and refreshing frozen sherbet. If you prefer, you could use plain yogurt in place of buttermilk, and blackcurrants instead of blueberries. Lemon verbena is easy to grow in a pot. The sprigs and leaves can be used both fresh and dried for infusing syrups for fruit compotes or salads, and also make a wonderfully refreshing herbal tea.

SERVES 4 TO 6

⅔ CUP GRANULATED SUGAR, PLUS EXTRA IF NEEDED, TO TASTE

2 STRIPS OF PEEL FROM A LEMON

SPRIG OF LEMON VERBENA

14 OUNCES BLUEBERRIES

SQUEEZE OF LEMON JUICE, TO TASTE (OPTIONAL)

1¾ CUPS BUTTERMILK

Equipment

FINE-MESH NYLON SIEVE

ICE-CREAM MAKER

PLASTIC FREEZER-SAFE CONTAINER

Put the sugar in a medium saucepan and add the lemon peel strips, lemon verbena, and ⅓ cup cold water. Slowly bring to a boil to dissolve the sugar, then simmer for 30 seconds. Remove from the heat and let stand at room temperature for 1 hour or so for the lemon peel and lemon verbena to infuse the syrup.

Strain the syrup, return to the pan, and bring back to a boil over medium heat. Add the blueberries and simmer for about 3 to 4 minutes to soften the berries. Remove from the heat, scoop out one-third of the berries, and reserve. Process the remainder to a purée using an immersion blender. Pass the purée through a fine-mesh nylon sieve, pressing on the fruit to extract as much flavor and fruit as possible. Taste the purée and add a little more sugar or a squeeze of lemon juice to balance the flavors.

Add the buttermilk and the reserved berries and mix until thoroughly combined. Cover with plastic wrap and chill in the fridge for 1 hour.

Churn the mixture in an ice-cream maker according to the manufacturer's instructions. Scoop the sherbet into a plastic freezer-safe container, cover, and freeze until firm before serving.

Blueberry and Almond Brioche Loaf

This is an impressive-looking loaf and one that is ideal to serve for brunch. You can prepare the first stage the night before and then simply assemble the loaf and let it rise the next morning. The method may seem rather long-winded, but I assure you it's simply a matter of plaiting the dough around the filling. As with most rich yeasted breads, this is best eaten on the day of making, but it will reheat quite happily the next day should you have leftovers.

SERVES 6 TO 8

½ CUP WHOLE MILK, PLUS EXTRA FOR BRUSHING

3 TABLESPOONS UNSALTED BUTTER AT ROOM TEMPERATURE, DICED

1¾ CUPS BREAD FLOUR, PLUS EXTRA FOR DUSTING

¼ OUNCE FAST-ACTION/EASY-BLEND DRIED YEAST

2 TABLESPOONS GRANULATED SUGAR, PLUS 1 TO 2 TABLESPOONS FOR SPRINKLING

A LARGE PINCH OF SALT

1 MEDIUM EGG, LIGHTLY BEATEN

SUNFLOWER OIL, FOR GREASING

7 OUNCES BLUEBERRIES

1 MEDIUM EGG WHITE

For the frangipane

1¼ CUPS GROUND ALMONDS

5 TABLESPOONS UNSALTED BUTTER, SOFTENED

⅓ CUP GRANULATED SUGAR

2 MEDIUM EGGS

3 TABLESPOONS ALL-PURPOSE FLOUR

FINELY GRATED ZEST OF ½ LEMON

1 TEASPOON VANILLA EXTRACT

A PINCH OF SALT

Warm the milk until it's just a shade warmer than hand hot, add the butter, and stir until melted. Thoroughly combine the flour, yeast, sugar, and salt with a balloon whisk before transferring everything into the bowl of a free-standing mixer fitted with a dough hook—this dough is quite soft and sticky, so it's easier to mix using a machine than by hand. Make a well in the middle of the dry ingredients and pour in the warm milk mixture. Add the beaten egg, mix well, and knead on a medium speed for 5 minutes until silky smooth and elastic.

Shape the dough into a ball, place in a lightly oiled large mixing bowl, and cover with plastic wrap. Leave in a warm, draft-free place for 1½ to 2 hours or until doubled in size. Alternatively, let rise overnight in the fridge.

Meanwhile, combine all the frangipane ingredients in a food processor until smooth.

Lightly dust the work surface with flour and knead the dough for 30 seconds to knock out any air pockets. On a large sheet of parchment paper, roll the dough out into a rectangle 16 × 12 inches and with one of the shorter sides closest to you. Mentally divide the dough into thirds from left to right and spread the frangipane into a neat, vertical rectangle in the middle third, leaving a ½ to 1-inch border at the top and bottom. Scatter the blueberries evenly over the frangipane. Take a sharp knife and, starting on the right-hand third, cut the dough into 12 strips running slightly diagonally down from the edge of the filling outward, leaving a ½ to 1-inch rectangle top and bottom. Repeat on the left-hand side, ensuring that the strips are equal in number and width to those on the right-hand side. Brush the dough with a little milk and fold the top and bottom rectangles over to seal. Starting with the strip on the top left-hand side, fold it over to encase the filling, followed by the top right-hand strip. Repeat all the way down the loaf, overlapping each strip as you go.

Slide the loaf, still on the parchment, onto a large baking sheet, loosely cover with oiled plastic wrap, and let rise in a warm place for 45 minutes to 1 hour or until almost doubled in size again.

Preheat the oven to 350°F. Beat the egg white until foamy, gently brush over the bread, and scatter with granulated sugar. Bake on the middle rack for 20 minutes, then reduce the temperature to 350°F and cook for another 10 to 15 minutes or until golden brown and well-risen. You may need to turn the pan around in the oven halfway through baking to ensure that the loaf browns evenly. Remove from the oven and cool on a wire rack.

Blueberry Pies

The dough in these individual pies is homemade puff pastry, which I am fully aware will have many people running for the chilled pastry section of the supermarket to seek out store-bought. I urge you to try homemade—it's far more delicious than anything from a package and made in a factory. And as the filling is very simple, your time can be wisely spent on making the pastry. You could also fill the pies with small, ripe cherries, a mixture of apples and blackberries, or peaches and blackcurrants.

MAKES 6 PIES

1 QUANTITY OF PUFF PASTRY DOUGH
(SEE PAGE 207)

ALL-PURPOSE FLOUR, FOR DUSTING

MILK, FOR BRUSHING

For the filling

14 OUNCES BLUEBERRIES

2 TO 3 TABLESPOONS GRANULATED SUGAR,
PLUS EXTRA FOR SPRINKLING

FINELY GRATED ZEST AND JUICE OF
½ LEMON

1 TABLESPOON CORNSTARCH

Equipment

6 × 5-INCH ROUND INDIVIDUAL TART PANS

For the filling, put half the blueberries into a small saucepan and add 1 tablespoon of the sugar and the lemon zest and juice. Cook over low to medium heat for about 3 minutes until the blueberries have started to burst and become juicy. Remove from the heat and add the remaining blueberries, the cornstarch, and the remaining 1 to 2 tablespoons of sugar to taste, then let cool.

Dust the work surface with flour and divide the pastry dough into thirds. Divide one-third of the dough into three even-sized pieces and roll each out into a circle, 1/16-inch thick. Line three of the tart pans with the dough, then use another third of the dough to line the remaining three pans. Spoon the blueberry filling evenly between the pie crusts.

For the pie tops, divide the last third of dough into six even portions and roll each out into a circle, 1/16-inch thick. Brush the inside edge of each pie crust with a little milk or water and place one top on each pie, pressing the edges to seal. Using a sharp knife, trim off any excess dough and use the back of the knife to crimp together the edges of the dough. Brush the tops with a little more milk and chill in the fridge for 30 minutes.

Preheat the oven to 350°F and place a solid baking sheet on the middle rack. Brush the tops of the tarts once again with milk and sprinkle with granulated sugar. Cut a small cross in the middle of each pie top and bake on the hot baking sheet for 30 minutes until the dough is puffed and golden and the filling bubbling.

Let the pies cool in the pans for 15 to 20 minutes and then serve warm with ice cream.

Berries with Rose, Cardamom, and Black Pepper Syrup

Dried rose petals are now widely available in larger supermarkets, online, or in Middle Eastern groceries. However, if you happen to grow deeply scented roses in your garden then a handful of petals—fresh or dried—would be a really lovely addition to this fruit compote. As always when using fresh flowers, ensure that they are clean, bug-free, and not sprayed with chemicals.

Homemade vanilla ice cream or a bowl of crème fraîche, Greek yogurt, or softly whipped heavy cream would be perfect alongside this dessert.

SERVES 4 TO 6

⅔ CUP GRANULATED SUGAR

A GOOD PINCH OF DRIED ROSE PETALS (FOOD GRADE)

½ TEASPOON BLACK PEPPERCORNS

3 CARDAMOM PODS

JUICE OF ½ LEMON

14 OUNCES STRAWBERRIES

5 OUNCES REDCURRANTS

11 OUNCES RASPBERRIES

5 FRESH FIGS, WASHED

Put the sugar into a saucepan and add ¾ cup of cold water and the rose petals. Using a mortar and pestle, very lightly crush the black peppercorns and cardamom pods and add to the pan. Set the pan over low to medium heat to gently dissolve the sugar. Bring to a boil, reduce to a simmer, and continue to cook gently for 2 minutes. Remove the syrup from the heat, add the lemon juice, and let cool and infuse with the petals and spices for 2 hours.

Hull and halve the strawberries and add to a serving bowl. Using a fork, strip the redcurrants from their stems directly into the bowl. Add the raspberries and figs, cut into slim wedges. Strain the syrup over the fruit, stir gently to combine, and leave for 30 minutes to 1 hour to allow the flavors to mingle before serving.

Seedless Raspberry Jelly

With its intense raspberry flavor and ruby-like shimmer, this jelly is not your everyday kind of spread. In fact, this would be just the thing to slather on top of the finest crumpets or scones for visiting VIP guests or royalty. And because it's rather special, this recipe doesn't make many jars. As well as a topping for scones, it makes a good filling for cakes, nutty or chocolate shortbreads, or macarons.

MAKES 4 JARS

1½ POUNDS RASPBERRIES

2 CUPS JAM SUGAR, OR USE GRANULATED AND
A SMALL HANDFUL OF REDCURRANTS
(SEE NOTE BELOW)

JUICE OF ½ LEMON

Equipment

STAINLESS STEEL PRESERVING PAN

JELLY STRAINER BAG OR LARGE PIECE OF
CLEAN CHEESECLOTH

4 × 9-OUNCE CANNING JARS

If you don't already own a jelly strainer bag, then I urge you to invest in one. They are relatively inexpensive, and once you're got the bug for making jellies and the like, you'll be hooked. I've used jam sugar for this recipe, which has a small amount of pectin already added, but if you can't find any, simply use granulated sugar and add a small handful of fresh redcurrants at the start of the recipe—they have a high pectin content that will help speed up the setting process.

Put the raspberries and ⅔ cup water into the pan and gently warm over low heat until the berries have broken down and released lots of scarlet-colored juice. Press and crush the fruit against the sides of the pan with a wooden spoon to encourage this process along, but don't allow the berries and juice to boil at this stage, as you want to preserve the fresh, vibrant raspberry flavor and color.

Pour the contents of the pan into a jelly strainer bag (or large piece of clean cheesecloth draped over a fine-mesh sieve) and suspend the bag over a clean bowl. I tie the loops of the jelly bag around the handles of a kitchen cupboard to get some elevation over the bowl. Let the juice drip slowly through the bag for at least 4 hours, but better still overnight. Don't be tempted to push, prod, squeeze, or poke the fruit, otherwise you'll end up with a cloudy juice that will produce a seedless jam rather than a crystal clear jelly. Once all of the juice has dripped through the bag you will be left with a bowl of scarlet juice and a jelly strainer bag of raspberry pulp. Discard the pulp.

Preheat the oven to 300°F. Measure the juice—you should have about 2 cups, but if you have less, make up the quantity with water. Pour into a clean saucepan, add the sugar and a tablespoon of the lemon juice, and bring slowly to a boil, stirring to completely dissolve the sugar. Cook at a steady boil for about 10 minutes, removing any foam that rises to the top of the juice with a slotted spoon, and then start testing to see if the jelly has reached setting point. Drop a teaspoonful of mixture onto a chilled saucer, leave it for 30 seconds to 1 minute, and then push it with the tip of your finger. If the jelly wrinkles, it's ready; if not, cook for another 3 minutes and then test for a set again.

Slide the pan off the heat, taste the jelly, and add a drop more lemon juice to sharpen the flavor if needed and remove any foam that might have formed. Ladle the jelly into a pitcher and then pour into hot, sterilized jars (see page 132), leaving ¼ to ½ inch headspace. Screw on the lids, process in a water bath (see page 40), and leave until completely cold before labeling and storing and in a cool, dark cupboard for up to 1 year. Once opened, store the jelly in the fridge and use within 1 month.

Raspberry, Pistachio and Passion Fruit Yo-Yos

As a child, I used to love a particular brand of jam sandwich cookies—they were filled with white buttercream and jam and each cookie had a smiley face imprinted on the surface. These are a more sophisticated spin on those old childhood favorites and are a perfect use for my Seedless Raspberry Jelly (see page 96).

MAKES 20

For the cookies

½ CUP SHELLED UNSALTED PISTACHIOS

12 TABLESPOONS UNSALTED BUTTER, SOFTENED

½ CUP CONFECTIONERS' SUGAR

1½ CUPS ALL-PURPOSE FLOUR

½ TEASPOON BAKING POWDER

⅓ CUP CORNSTARCH

A PINCH OF SALT

2 TABLESPOONS STRAINED PASSION FRUIT JUICE OR MILK

For the filling

2½ OUNCES WHITE CHOCOLATE, CHOPPED

5 TABLESPOONS UNSALTED BUTTER, SOFTENED

1¼ CUPS CONFECTIONERS' SUGAR

2 PASSION FRUIT, HALVED WITH SEEDS AND PULP SCOOPED OUT

20 TEASPOONS SEEDLESS RASPBERRY JELLY (SEE PAGE 96)

Preheat the oven to 350°F and line two baking sheets with parchment paper.

Make the cookies first: Very finely chop the pistachios—you will find this easier and quicker if you have a mini chopper, or chop in a food processor. Cream the butter and confectioners' sugar until very pale and fluffy—this will take about 4 minutes using a free-standing mixer. Sift in the dry ingredients, add the chopped pistachios and passion fruit juice or milk, and mix well until smooth.

Break off large, cherry-sized nuggets of dough, roll into smooth balls, and arrange on the prepared baking sheets—you should have 40 balls. Dip the tines of a fork into cold water and firmly press into the top of each cookie to flatten slightly (the water helps to stop the dough from sticking to the tines). Bake on the middle rack of the oven for about 12 minutes until pale golden, swapping the pans around halfway through the baking time to ensure that they color evenly. Let cool on the pans.

To make the filling, melt the chocolate in a heatproof bowl, either in the microwave in short bursts on a low setting or over a saucepan of barely simmering water. Stir until smooth and let cool slightly.

Cream the butter and confectioners' sugar until smooth, pale, and light. Add the passion fruit and melted chocolate and beat until smooth and spreadable.

Spread the underside of 20 of the cookies with a teaspoon of filling and the remaining cookies with the raspberry jelly. Sandwich the two together and serve with a smile!

Raspberry Tarts

Elegant enough to be served at the most fancy afternoon tea party, these little tartlets have a double hit of raspberry. The filling is a rich raspberry custard, which is then topped with a layer of Seedless Raspberry Jelly (see page 96). But if you don't have the inclination to make the jelly, a good raspberry jam will suffice.

MAKES 12

For the dough

1½ CUPS ALL-PURPOSE FLOUR, PLUS EXTRA FOR DUSTING

¼ CUP CONFECTIONERS' SUGAR, PLUS EXTRA FOR DUSTING

A PINCH OF SALT

9 TABLESPOONS UNSALTED BUTTER, CHILLED AND DICED

1 MEDIUM EGG YOLK

2 TABLESPOONS ICED WATER

2 TEASPOONS LEMON JUICE

For the filling

12 OUNCES RASPBERRIES, PLUS EXTRA TO SERVE

SQUEEZE OF LEMON JUICE

½ TO ⅔ CUP GRANULATED SUGAR, PLUS 2 TABLESPOONS

1 MEDIUM EGG

3 MEDIUM EGG YOLKS

½ CUP HEAVY CREAM OR CRÈME FRAÎCHE

To serve

6 TABLESPOONS SEEDLESS RASPBERRY JELLY (SEE PAGE 96)

CRÈME FRAÎCHE

EDIBLE FLOWERS

Equipment

FINE-MESH NYLON SIEVE

12 TARTLET PANS

5-INCH PLAIN COOKIE CUTTER

Put the flour in the bowl of a food processor, add the confectioners' sugar and salt, and pulse briefly to combine. Then add the butter and pulse briefly again until just incorporated. Pour the mixture into a mixing bowl and make a well in the middle. Add the egg yolk, iced water, and lemon juice and, using a round-bladed bread-and-butter knife, cut through the mixture to combine the ingredients and bring the dough together. Use your hands to very lightly knead the dough and to form it into a neat ball, but try not to overwork the dough or the resulting tart crust will be tough rather than light and crumbly. Flatten the dough into a disc, cover with plastic wrap, and chill in the fridge for 2 hours.

Next, make the filling: Place the raspberries in a small saucepan with the lemon juice, 2 tablespoons of the granulated sugar and a splash of water. Cook over low heat for about 6 minutes until the fruit is very soft and the purée just starts to thicken. Push through a fine-mesh nylon sieve into a bowl. Add the remaining sugar, the quantity depending on how naturally sweet the purée is, and let cool for 10 minutes. Beat the whole egg and egg yolks together and add to the purée with the cream or crème fraîche and whisk to combine. Strain through the sieve into a bowl and set aside.

Lightly dust the work surface with flour and roll the dough out to a thickness of no more than 1/16-inch. Stamp out discs from the dough with the cutter and use to line the tartlet pans, pressing the dough into the corners. Prick the bottoms and chill the tart crusts in the fridge for 15 minutes while you preheat the oven to 350°F. Line each tart crust with foil and fill with baking beans or uncooked rice, arrange on a baking sheet, and bake on the middle rack of the oven for 10 to 12 minutes until pale golden. Remove the foil and baking beans or rice and divide the filling between the tart crusts. Return to the oven for another 12 to 13 minutes until the filling has set. Leave until completely cold and then chill in the fridge until firm.

Warm the raspberry jelly in a small saucepan and brush over the top of each tart. Decorate the tarts with a small dollop of crème fraîche, extra raspberries, edible flowers, and a light dusting of confectioners' sugar.

Summer Berry Tiramisu Cake

This is a real show-stopper cake—something to make for an occasion when you have a little time and berries and currants are plentiful. It's not tricky to make but does require concentration—and a crowd to feed. The filling is a twist on zabaglione, which on its own would be delicious—even without the mascarpone and white chocolate—served warm over macerated berries or sliced peaches. I have chosen to make this cake an impressive six-layered affair, but it can just as easily be left as a more manageable three tiers. You may have some filling left over, which can be served alongside.

SERVES 8 TO 10

For the cake layers

3 TABLESPOONS UNSALTED BUTTER, MELTED AND SLIGHTLY COOLED, PLUS EXTRA FOR GREASING

1¼ CUPS ALL-PURPOSE FLOUR, PLUS EXTRA FOR DUSTING

6 LARGE EGGS

¾ CUP GRANULATED SUGAR

1 TEASPOON VANILLA EXTRACT

½ CUP GROUND ALMONDS

1 TEASPOON BAKING POWDER

A PINCH OF SALT

For the mascarpone filling

4 LARGE EGG YOLKS

¼ CUP GRANULATED SUGAR

2 TABLESPOONS Marsala

A PINCH OF SALT

FINELY GRATED ZEST OF 1 LEMON

2 CUPS MASCARPONE, BEATEN UNTIL SMOOTH

3½ OUNCES WHITE CHOCOLATE, CHOPPED AND MELTED

For the macerated berries

1¾ POUNDS MIXED BERRIES AND CURRANTS, PLUS EXTRA TO SERVE

1 TABLESPOON LEMON JUICE

1 TABLESPOON GRANULATED SUGAR

½ TEASPOON VANILLA EXTRACT

3 TABLESPOONS Marsala

CONFECTIONERS' SUGAR, FOR DUSTING

Equipment

3 × 8-INCH SANDWICH CAKE PANS

Preheat the oven to 350°F. Grease the inside of the cake pans and line the bottoms with discs of greased parchment paper. Lightly dust the insides of the pans with flour and tap out the excess.

Using a free-standing mixer fitted with a whisk attachment, whisk the eggs, sugar, and vanilla together on medium-high speed until very thick and pale, tripled in volume, and the mixture leaves a ribbon trail when the whisk is lifted from the bowl. Sift in the dry ingredients and, using a large metal spoon, gently fold in. Pour the melted butter around the edges of the bowl and gently fold in.

Divide the batter evenly between the prepared pans—I carefully weigh the mixture to ensure that my cakes are 100% even—spread level and bake on the middle rack of the oven for 18 to 20 minutes or until golden, well-risen, and a wooden skewer inserted into the middle comes out clean. Let cool in the pans for a couple of minutes, then transfer to a wire rack to cool completely.

For the filling, whisk the egg yolks, sugar, Marsala, and salt in a heatproof glass or ceramic bowl set over a saucepan of simmering water. Continue whisking for 5 minutes or until the mixture is hot to the touch, very thick, tripled in volume, and the consistency of softly whipped cream. Remove from the heat and plunge the base of the bowl into cold water to cool, add the lemon zest, and whisk until cold. Fold in the mascarpone and melted chocolate.

Place the berries, lemon juice, sugar, and vanilla in a bowl and stir to coat. Let macerate for 10 minutes.

Using a bread knife, slice each cake in half horizontally. Choose the best-looking top slice and set aside. Lay the remaining slices on the work surface and drizzle with the Marsala. Divide the filling between the slices, spreading it almost to the edge. Place one of the bottom layers on a serving plate and scatter with one-fifth of the berries. Top with a second layer and more berries. Continue layering in this manner, finishing with the reserved layer. Gently press the layers together, cover loosely with plastic wrap, and chill for 1 hour. Serve with a pile of extra berries on top and a light dusting of confectioners' sugar.

Summer Berry Trifles

This elegant dessert has all the classic elements of a trifle but assembled in a looser, free-form fashion. Although this recipe has a number of stages, each part can be prepared in advance and plated just before serving.

SERVES 6

For the jelly

9 OUNCES HULLED STRAWBERRIES, SLICED

7 OUNCES RASPBERRIES

2 TABLESPOONS GRANULATED SUGAR, PLUS EXTRA TO TASTE

A SQUEEZE OF LEMON JUICE

2 SHEETS OF PLATINUM-GRADE LEAF GELATIN

For the cake

3 MEDIUM EGGS

½ CUP GRANULATED SUGAR

1 TEASPOON FINELY GRATED LEMON ZEST

⅓ CUP ALL-PURPOSE FLOUR, PLUS EXTRA FOR DUSTING

½ CUP GROUND ALMONDS

1 TEASPOON BAKING POWDER

A PINCH OF SALT

3 TABLESPOONS UNSALTED BUTTER, MELTED AND SLIGHTLY COOLED, PLUS EXTRA FOR GREASING

8 TEASPOONS SEEDLESS RASPBERRY JELLY (SEE PAGE 96) OR RASPBERRY JAM

For the custard

¾ CUP FULL-FAT MILK

⅓ CUP GRANULATED SUGAR

3 LARGE EGG YOLKS

1 LEVEL TABLESPOON CORNSTARCH

1 TEASPOON VANILLA BEAN PASTE

¾ CUP HEAVY CREAM, WHIPPED UNTIL THICK BUT STILL FLOPPY

For the berries

⅓ CUP GRANULATED SUGAR

1 TABLESPOON FOOD-GRADE DRIED ROSE PETALS OR 1 TEASPOON ROSEWATER

A GOOD SQUEEZE OF LEMON JUICE

7 OUNCES RASPBERRIES

3½ OUNCES BLUEBERRIES

7 OUNCES STRAWBERRIES, HULLED AND QUARTERED

Equipment

FINE-MESH NYLON SIEVE

5½ × 8-INCH BAKING PAN OR PLASTIC FREEZER CONTAINER LINED WITH PLASTIC WRAP

12 × 16-INCH SWISS ROLL OR BAKING PAN

1½ TO 2-INCH PLAIN COOKIE CUTTER

For the jelly, heat the berries, sugar, lemon juice, and ¼ cup of cold water in a saucepan over low heat to dissolve the sugar and soften the fruit. Continue to heat gently for 10 minutes or until the berries completely break down and release their juices. Pour into a fine-mesh nylon sieve over a bowl and let the juice drip through, without pressing the fruit—this can take up to 4 hours. Measure the juice—you should have about 1 cup—and add enough water to make up to 1¼ cups. Taste and add more sugar if needed.

Soak the gelatin sheets in a bowl of cold water for 10 minutes until soft. Heat half the berry juice in a small saucepan to just below boiling, then remove from the heat. Drain the gelatin sheets, squeeze out any excess water, add to the hot juice, and whisk to combine. Add the remaining juice, whisk again, and pour into the plastic wrap-lined pan or container. Let cool, then cover and chill in the fridge for at least 2 hours until set.

Meanwhile, preheat the oven to 350°F. Line the baking pan with greased parchment paper, lightly dust with flour, and tap out the excess. Using a free-standing mixer fitted with a whisk attachment, whisk the eggs and sugar until thick, pale, and doubled in volume. Add the lemon zest and whisk again. Sift in the dry ingredients and fold in using a large metal spoon. Pour the melted butter around the edges of the bowl and gently fold in. Carefully spoon into the prepared pan and spread level. Bake on the middle rack for 9 to 10 minutes until golden and firm to the touch. Let cool in the pan.

Using the cookie cutter, stamp out 24 discs from the cake. Spread 12 with the raspberry jelly or jam and sandwich with the remaining discs.

For the custard, bring the milk to a boil in a saucepan. In a bowl, whisk together the sugar, egg yolks, cornstarch, and vanilla. Pour the hot milk over and whisk constantly until smooth and thoroughly combined. Return to the pan and cook gently, whisking constantly, until thickened and you can no longer taste the cornstarch. Pour through a fine-mesh sieve into a clean bowl, cover the surface with plastic wrap, and leave until cold. Chill for at least 2 hours. Fold in the whipped cream.

For the berries, bring ⅓ cup water, the sugar, rose petals or rosewater, and lemon juice to a boil in a small pan until the sugar has dissolved, remove from the heat, and let infuse for 1 hour. Strain into another pan, discarding the rose petals, if using, and bring back to a boil, then remove from the heat and add the berries. Let infuse for 1 hour.

To serve, turn the jelly out and cut into neat dice. Spoon 2 tablespoons of custard into each bowl, scatter with the diced jelly, and arrange 2 little sandwich cakes to one side. Top with a spoonful of berries and a drizzle of rose-scented syrup and serve immediately.

Pistachio, Coconut, and Lime Cake

This is one of my all-time favorite cakes—and that's saying something for a chocolate cake fiend! Serve it on the day of baking or make it the day ahead; either way, it's pretty darn good. There's just enough coconut for you to know it's there, but not so much that it overpowers the tangy lime and nutty pistachio. Drizzled with just enough syrup to moisten the cake without drowning it and making it heavy, and accompanied by gently softened, lime-infused berries and a spoonful of cool fromage frais or crème fraîche, it's just as good served as a dessert as it is an afternoon snack.

If you happen to find a bottle of pistachio oil in your local deli, then grab it and use it in this recipe. It has a wonderful nutty flavor and aroma that hits you the moment you unscrew the cap—it's pricey but can also be used to make a delicious pesto salad dressing (see page 147). I try also to use sliced pistachios, which have had their purple skins removed. They are available from Middle Eastern supermarkets and specialty online food suppliers.

SERVES 8 TO 10

For the cake

5 TABLESPOONS UNSALTED BUTTER, SOFTENED, PLUS EXTRA FOR GREASING

⅓ CUP OLIVE OR PISTACHIO OIL

1¼ CUP SHELLED UNSALTED PISTACHIOS

½ CUP UNSWEETENED SHREDDED COCONUT

1 CUP ALL-PURPOSE FLOUR

2 TEASPOONS BAKING POWDER

A PINCH OF SALT

4 MEDIUM EGGS

1 CUP GRANULATED SUGAR

FINELY GRATED ZEST OF 2 LIMES

3 ROUNDED TABLESPOONS SOUR CREAM

For the syrup

FRESHLY SQUEEZED JUICE OF 3 LIMES

5 TABLESPOONS AGAVE SYRUP OR MILD-TASTING HONEY

3 TABLESPOONS GRANULATED SUGAR

7 OUNCES BLUEBERRIES

7 OUNCES BLACKBERRIES

NATURAL FROMAGE FRAIS, CRÈME FRAÎCHE, OR GREEK YOGURT, TO SERVE

Equipment

9-INCH SPRINGFORM CAKE PAN

Preheat the oven to 325°F. Grease the pan and line the bottom with parchment paper.

Melt the butter with the olive or pistachio oil in a small saucepan over low heat. Remove from the heat and let cool slightly.

Blend the pistachios in a food processor until they are very finely chopped. Add the coconut, flour, baking powder, and salt and process for no more than 10 seconds, just to combine.

Using an electric mixer, whisk the eggs and sugar on medium to high speed until they are very thick and pale, tripled in volume, and leave a ribbon trail when the whisk is lifted from the bowl. Gently fold in the lime zest and pistachio mixture using a large metal spoon, then fold in the butter mixture and sour cream. Pour into the pan, spread level, and bake on the middle rack of the oven for 40 to 50 minutes or until a wooden skewer inserted into the middle comes out clean.

Meanwhile, prepare the syrup: In a small saucepan, bring the lime juice, agave syrup or honey, sugar, and ¼ cup of cold water to a boil. Continue to bubble steadily until reduced by half and syrupy.

Let the cake cool in the pan on a wire rack for 5 minutes, then carefully run an offset palette knife around the edges of the cake to release the sides from the pan. Using the wooden skewer, make holes all over the top of the cake, then while it is still in the pan either slowly drizzle or carefully brush half the syrup all over the warm cake. Set aside until completely cold.

Pour the berries into the remaining syrup and return to low heat for a couple of minutes to slightly soften them. Remove from the heat, spoon into a bowl, and let cool.

Serve the cake in slices with fromage frais, crème fraîche, or Greek yogurt and the berry compote spooned over.

Stone

As summer rolls along, nature provides us with yet another staggering array of fruits, with cherries, peaches, nectarines, plums, and apricots being possibly my best loved of all. As delicious eaten raw as they are cooked, and shining in both savory and sweet dishes, stone fruits earn their rightful place in my kitchen and cooking, whether in salads and bakes, drinks and preserves, or in decadent ice creams and refreshing popsicles and sorbets.

A bag of fully ripe, glistening dark purple cherries is like a bag of treasure. If you are anything like me and you're cooking a dish that calls for fresh cherries, you'll need to buy twice as many as the recipe requires, as they are impossible to resist. I will certainly have eaten handfuls before getting anywhere near the kitchen.

As high summer kicks in, so does the peach and nectarine season. Peaches—yellow or white-fleshed, round or donut-shaped—are one of those fruits that I seem to almost overdose on during the summer months. I spent years living in South West France where we had a small peach tree in the garden, but size was not an issue when it came to the quantity of fruit that this one modest tree yielded. As all of some 200 peaches ripened in a couple of weeks, we cooked up jams, preserves, syrups, and chutneys to make the most of the crop and not waste a single fruit. I still adore large yellow-fleshed peaches despite the fruit frenzy that I associate with them.

Perfect apricots with their slightly downy skin and shape that makes me think of an angel's bottom seem to come to life when cooked—even less-than-perfect apricots can be transformed with a little heat and sugar. The same applies to plums—even slightly underripe specimens when cut in half, sprinkled with sugar, and baked in a medium oven become a delicious affair that can be served straight up or puréed and churned in an ice-cream maker for one of my favorite sorbets.

All varieties of stone fruit make wonderful jams and preserves. I prefer my jam slightly less sweet than is traditional, resulting in a slightly softer set and shorter shelf life, but this allows the bright flavor of the fruit to really shine through. I also make jams in smaller batches, which is partly due to my desire to make the most of the season's offerings and variety, but also so that I can fill my cupboards with a wider selection of flavors without feeling overwhelmed by one type.

Bulgur Wheat Salad with Cherries and Feta

This is the kind of food that I love most—fresh and full of flavor. It's ideal for those lazy outdoor summer lunches, when you really don't want to stand in the hot kitchen for longer than necessary. And it tastes even better the next day. Serve with Lamb Kofte (see page 114), simply barbecued lamb chops, or a za'atar-crusted rack of lamb or fish—or just with some warm flatbreads and a bowl of hummus.

SERVES 4 TO 6

1¾ CUPS BULGUR WHEAT

SALT AND FRESHLY GROUND BLACK PEPPER

½ CUP WHOLE ALMONDS

¾ CUP FLAT-LEAF PARSLEY

½ CUP FRESH MINT

½ CUP FRESH CILANTRO

2½ CUPS ARUGULA

1 HEAD OF FENNEL

5 SCALLIONS

A HANDFUL OF RADISHES

1 SMALL LEBANESE CUCUMBER OR
½ REGULAR CUCUMBER

JUICE OF 1 LEMON, OR TO TASTE

4 TO 5 TABLESPOONS FRUITY OLIVE OIL,
OR TO TASTE

9 OUNCES CHERRIES, WASHED AND DRIED

1 CUP FETA

A GOOD PINCH OF GROUND SUMAC
(OPTIONAL)

Wash the bulgur wheat in a strainer under cold running water. Transfer to a pan, cover with 4 cups of cold water, and add a pinch of salt. Bring to a boil, half cover, and simmer for about 15 minutes until tender. Drain and refresh under cold running water. Let drain in the strainer while you prepare the remaining ingredients.

Toast the almonds either in a dry frying pan over medium heat—shaking the pan to prevent the nuts from scorching—or in the oven on a baking sheet for 3 to 4 minutes if you happen to have it on already. When cool enough to handle, cut into slivers.

Chop the parsley, mint, cilantro, and arugula—how finely you chop the herbs depends on your preference, but I usually go for coarsely chopped—and add to a large bowl. Trim the fennel, cut into quarters through the root, and cut out the tough core from each wedge. Finely slice and add to the herbs. Trim and finely chop the scallions. Wash and trim the radishes and finely slice or cut into matchsticks. Wash the cucumber, trim the ends, and cut into small dice. Add all to the bowl.

Squeeze out any remaining water from the bulgur wheat and pour into the bowl. Add the lemon juice and olive oil, season well with salt and black pepper, and mix to combine.

Now for the cherries. Taking one at a time, remove the stem and, holding it over the salad bowl, squeeze it between your fingers to pop out the pit—this way, the cherry juice drips into the salad and isn't wasted. Break the cherry flesh into rough pieces and add to the bowl. Crumble the feta over the top, add the almonds, and mix gently to combine.

This salad tastes best an hour or so after making, once all the flavors have mingled. After this time, taste the salad and add more oil, lemon juice, salt, or pepper if needed. Sprinkle with the sumac, if using, and serve.

Lamb Kofte with Cherries

I love simple, super-tasty dishes that are perfect for sharing. These little meatballs make an ideal light lunch, or can be served as part of a bigger spread and would be wonderful with my Bulgur Wheat Salad with Cherries and Feta on page 112. Here, these kofte are served with grilled flatbreads, snappy pickled red onion, pickled green chiles, a cooling tahini sauce, and fresh cucumbers. But as an alternative, try adding a can of good-quality chopped tomatoes to the pan of browned kofte, enough stock to just cover, and a dash of pomegranate molasses, then cover and cook for 30 minutes in a medium oven.

SERVES 4

2 TABLESPOONS OLIVE OIL

1 SMALL ONION, FINELY CHOPPED

1 FAT GARLIC CLOVE, FINELY CHOPPED

½ CUP PINE NUTS

½ CUP FLAT-LEAF PARSLEY, FINELY CHOPPED

½ CUP FRESH MINT, FINELY CHOPPED

1 GREEN CHILE, SEEDED AND FINELY CHOPPED

½ TEASPOON GROUND CUMIN

¼ TEASPOON GROUND ALLSPICE

¼ TEASPOON GROUND CINNAMON

5 OUNCES CHERRIES, WASHED

14 OUNCES LEAN GROUND LAMB

SALT AND FRESHLY GROUND BLACK PEPPER

For the pickled red onion

1 RED ONION, THINLY SLICED

2 TABLESPOONS WHITE WINE VINEGAR

2 TEASPOONS GRANULATED SUGAR

A PINCH OF SALT

For the tahini sauce

1 FAT GARLIC CLOVE, CRUSHED

2 TABLESPOONS TAHINI PASTE

¼ CUP GREEK YOGURT

JUICE OF ½ LEMON, OR TO TASTE

½ TEASPOON GROUND CUMIN

To serve

GRILLED FLATBREADS

SMALL LEBANESE CUCUMBERS

PICKLED GREEN CHILES

LEMON WEDGES

Heat 1 tablespoon of the olive oil in a small saucepan, add the onion, and cook gently for about 3 minutes until soft but not colored. Add the garlic and cook for another minute. Transfer to a bowl. Lightly toast the pine nuts in the same pan, shaking them to ensure that they brown evenly without scorching, and add to the onion and garlic. Add the herbs and chile to the bowl along with the spices. Remove the stem from each cherry and, holding it over the bowl to catch any juices, squeeze it between your fingers to pop out the pit. Coarsely chop the cherry flesh and add to the bowl with the ground lamb. Season well with salt and black pepper and, using your hands, mix and knead the mixture to thoroughly combine. Shape into neat golf ball-sized balls.

Preheat the oven to 375°F. Heat the remaining tablespoon of olive oil in a frying pan over medium heat and cook the kofte in batches for about 3 minutes, turning them frequently so that they brown well on all sides. Transfer to an ovenproof dish or baking sheet and keep warm in the oven while you prepare the pickled red onion and the sauce.

Toss the red onion in a glass or ceramic bowl with the vinegar, sugar, and salt and leave for 20 minutes to soften and lightly pickle. In a small bowl, mix together all the ingredients for the tahini sauce with enough water until smooth and the consistency of very softly whipped cream. Taste and add salt and/or more lemon juice to taste.

Serve the kofte hot with the pickled red onion, tahini sauce, grilled flatbreads, cucumber wedges, pickled green chiles, and lemon wedges to squeeze over the top.

Cherry Cordial

Now here's a hard-working bottle of goodness. Not only does this cordial make deliciously refreshing soft drinks and ice pops when diluted with still or sparkling water, it can be stirred through yogurt, drizzled over pancakes, and makes a mighty fine addition to that retro burger bar classic Coke Float: drop a scoop of vanilla ice cream into a tall glass and top with Coca-Cola and a drizzle of cherry cordial. Or keep it simple and serve a generous glug of cordial over vanilla or chocolate ice cream. However, even better and for a more adult theme, try adding some to your summer cocktail experiments. A splash of cordial and a dash of cherry brandy will give some extra oomph to a glass of inferior sparkling wine. And if you were to thicken the syrup, soften the cherries and reduce the syrup a little further, it would be rather wonderful to spoon the warm syrup and sticky cherries over rich, dark chocolate brownies. Add a good dollop of softly whipped cream and I think I might be swooning.

MAKES ABOUT 2½ CUPS

1¾ POUNDS CHERRIES, WASHED

½ VANILLA BEAN, SPLIT IN HALF
LENGTHWISE

1¼ CUPS GRANULATED SUGAR

JUICE OF ½ LEMON

Equipment

FINE-MESH NYLON SIEVE

2 × 12-OUNCE BOTTLES

ICE POP MOLDS (OPTIONAL)

Remove the stem from each cherry and cut in half. Using your fingers, remove the pits and put the fruit in a mixing bowl. This might seem a labor-intensive way to remove the pits but it's really quite satisfying. Add the vanilla bean to the bowl with the sugar and lemon juice. Stir well, cover, and leave at room temperature for at least 1 hour to allow the sugar to completely dissolve and to draw the juice from the cherries.

Scoop the mixture into a saucepan, add 1 cup cold water, and place over low heat. Bring to a boil and then simmer for 3 to 4 minutes. Pour through a fine-mesh nylon sieve into a pitcher and leave for a couple of hours for every last drop to drip through. Pour into sterilized bottles (see page 132), seal, and store in the fridge until needed. It will keep for up to 6 weeks.

To make ice pop, dilute the cordial to taste and then add a drop more cordial—this instruction may seem contradictory, but as the cordial freezes it will lose a little sweetness and flavor, so you'll need to add a bit extra to compensate for this. Pour into ice pop molds and freeze until solid. Perfect on a balmy summer's day.

You can also make this cordial using strawberries in place of cherries—add a handful of pineapple mint leaves for a further twist.

Cherry and Almond Crumble Cake

This cake has a number of elements that at first glance might look a little intimidating, but bear with me. It received a big thumbs-up from my harshest critic and chief taste tester who felt that all the various layers were necessary—and Mom knows best. On the bottom is a buttery shortbread base, topped with a layer of cherry jam, followed by a rich almond cake studded with fresh juicy cherries that are almost hidden under a crisp crumble topping. If you want to make life one little step easier, you could leave out the crumble layer and simply scatter the top of the cake with sliced or chopped almonds. It's equally good served slightly warm as a dessert, with vanilla ice cream.

SERVES 8 TO 10

For the shortbread base

7 TABLESPOONS UNSALTED BUTTER, CHILLED
AND DICED, PLUS EXTRA FOR GREASING

1 CUP ALL-PURPOSE FLOUR

¼ CUP CONFECTIONERS' SUGAR

A PINCH OF SALT

3 TABLESPOONS CHERRY JAM

For the crumble topping

½ CUP SLICED ALMONDS

¼ CUP LIGHT BROWN SUGAR

⅓ CUP ALL-PURPOSE FLOUR

2 TABLESPOONS UNSALTED BUTTER, MELTED

For the cake

9 TABLESPOONS UNSALTED BUTTER,
SOFTENED

⅔ CUP GRANULATED SUGAR

3 MEDIUM EGGS, BEATEN

1 TEASPOON FINELY GRATED LEMON ZEST

1 TEASPOON VANILLA BEAN PASTE
OR EXTRACT

¼ TEASPOON ALMOND EXTRACT

1 CUP GROUND ALMONDS

⅔ CUP ALL-PURPOSE FLOUR

1 TEASPOON BAKING POWDER

A PINCH OF SALT

2 TABLESPOONS SOUR CREAM

12 OUNCES CHERRIES, PITTED

Equipment

8-INCH SPRINGFORM CAKE PAN

Preheat the oven to 350°F. Grease the cake pan and line the bottom with parchment paper.

Prepare the shortbread base first: In a food processor, pulse together the butter, flour, confectioners' sugar, and salt until the butter has been rubbed into the flour. Place into the prepared pan and press into an even layer covering the base. If your jam is a tad chunky, give it a few quick pulses in the food processor to break up any large bits.

Bake the shortbread on the middle rack of the oven for 12 minutes until pale golden. Let cool in the pan on a wire rack.

Place the dry ingredients for the crumble topping in a bowl and stir in the melted butter with your fingertips until the mixture starts to clump together.

Now for the cake: Cream the butter and sugar until really pale and light. Gradually add the beaten eggs, mixing well between each addition and scraping down the sides of the bowl with a rubber spatula from time to time. Add the lemon zest, vanilla, and almond extract and mix again. Sift in the dry ingredients and beat until smooth, then add the sour cream and mix again.

Spread the jam evenly over the shortbread, leaving a ½-inch border around the edges so it doesn't burn on the sides of the pan. Spoon over the cake mixture and spread level, arrange the cherries on top, and scatter with the crumble. Bake on the middle rack of the oven for 45 minutes to 1 hour until golden brown, well-risen, and a skewer inserted into the middle comes out clean. Loosely cover the top with parchment paper if it appears to be browning too quickly.

Let the cake cool in the pan for 10 minutes, then run a palette knife around the edges to loosen the sides, remove from the pan, and cool completely on a wire rack.

Chocolate, Cherry, and Turrón Ice Cream

Turrón is almond nougat that hails from Spain, while *torrone* is the Italian version and can be found in hard (*duro*) or soft (*morbido*) varieties; for this recipe you'll need hard nougat. The cherry compote stirred though this rich chocolate ice cream is literally the cherry on the top—the combination of cherries, chocolate, and almonds is the stuff of dreams.

SERVES 6 TO 8

1¼ CUPS WHOLE MILK

1½ CUPS HEAVY CREAM

1 TABLESPOON COCOA POWDER

3 MEDIUM EGG YOLKS

1 CUP GRANULATED SUGAR

1 TEASPOON VANILLA EXTRACT

A PINCH OF SALT

6 OUNCES DARK CHOCOLATE, FINELY CHOPPED

For the cherry compote and nougat

14 OUNCES RIPE DARK CHERRIES, WASHED

½ CUP GRANULATED SUGAR

JUICE OF ½ LEMON

5 OUNCES HARD ALMOND NOUGAT (TURRÓN OR TORRONE)

WAFFLE CONES, TO SERVE

Equipment

ICE-CREAM MAKER

PLASTIC FREEZER-SAFE CONTAINER

Pour the milk and half the cream into a medium saucepan, add the cocoa, and whisk to combine. Bring to a boil over medium heat. Meanwhile, using a hand-held mixer, beat the egg yolks, sugar, vanilla, and salt in a bowl until pale, smooth, and light. Steadily pour over 3 to 4 tablespoons of the hot milk mixture and beat constantly until smooth. Add the remaining milk mixture and beat until combined. Return to the pan and cook over low heat, stirring constantly, for about 3 minutes until the mixture thickens enough to coat the back of a spoon—don't let it boil or the eggs will scramble.

Put the chopped chocolate in a bowl, pour the hot custard on top in a steady stream, and whisk constantly until smooth and the chocolate has thoroughly melted. Add the remaining cream and whisk until silky smooth. Leave until cold and then cover and chill for at least 4 hours or overnight.

Meanwhile, prepare the cherry compote and nougat: Remove the stem from each cherry and, holding it over a small saucepan to catch the juice, squeeze it between your fingers to pop out the pit. Very coarsely chop the cherry flesh and add to the pan along with the sugar, lemon juice, and ¼ cup cold water. Set over low heat and stir constantly until the sugar has dissolved, then simmer gently for about 20 minutes until the cherries have softened and the juice is very thick and syrupy. Let cool. Cut the nougat into small dice.

Churn the chocolate custard in the ice-cream maker according to the manufacturer's instructions. Scoop into a plastic freezer-safe container, add the cherry compote and nougat, mix to combine, and freeze until firm.

Serve generous scoops of the ice cream in waffle cones.

Dried Cherry and Hazelnut Wafers for Cheese

These wafers are a cross between savory biscotti and Melba toast, with a nod and a wink to soda bread along the way. I love dried sour cherries and am always looking for new ways to use them—normally they crop up in my sweet baking, but they pair especially well with nuts and creamy, almost grassy-tasting fresh goat cheese.

MAKES ABOUT 30 TO 40

UNSALTED BUTTER, FOR GREASING

¾ CUP WHOLE BLANCHED HAZELNUTS

2½ OUNCES DRIED SOUR CHERRIES

1⅔ CUPS ALL-PURPOSE FLOUR

1¼ CUPS WHOLE-GRAIN SPELT FLOUR

½ TEASPOON BAKING POWDER

1 TEASPOON BAKING SODA

A GOOD PINCH OF SEA SALT

A GOOD GRINDING OF BLACK PEPPER

2 TABLESPOONS BROWN SUGAR

½ CUP MIXED SEEDS, SUCH AS SUNFLOWER, PUMPKIN, AND LINSEED

1 CUP BUTTERMILK

2 TABLESPOONS EXTRA VIRGIN OLIVE OIL

1 TABLESPOON HONEY

Equipment

2-POUND LOAF PAN

Preheat the oven to 350°F. Grease and line the bottom and sides of the loaf pan with a strip of greased parchment paper.

Pour the hazelnuts onto a baking sheet and toast in the oven for 4 minutes until pale golden. Let cool, then very coarsely chop. Coarsely chop the dried sour cherries if they are large.

Sift the flours, baking powder, baking soda, salt, and pepper into a large mixing bowl. Add the sugar, hazelnuts, dried cherries, and seeds and mix to combine. In a bowl, mix together the buttermilk, olive oil, and honey. Add to the dry ingredients and mix well until combined, then use your hands to very lightly knead and bring the dough together until almost smooth.

Pat the dough into a rectangle slightly smaller than the pan and press into the pan to fill it right into the corners. Bake on the middle rack of the oven for 35 to 40 minutes until risen, firm, and golden. Let cool in the pan for 3 to 4 minutes and then turn onto a wire rack until completely cold—about 4 hours. In the meantime, turn the oven off.

Preheat to the oven to 300°F. Using a long, serrated bread knife, cut the loaf into slices no thicker than ¹⁄₁₆-inch and arrange on parchment paper-covered baking sheets. Bake in batches for 10 to 15 minutes on the middle rack, swapping the pans around so that they cook evenly, until crisp and very lightly toasted.

Cool on wire racks before serving or storing in an airtight container until ready to eat—they will keep for up to 2 weeks.

Plum Ravioli

Feather-light pastries, filled with homemade plum compote, deep-fried, and dusted heavily with confectioners' sugar—I challenge you to eat just one! I have kept the sugar in the plum compote to a minimum, which makes it sharp and fruity and a nice contrast to the dough and confectioners' sugar, but if you have an especially sweet tooth you may want to increase it.

MAKES ABOUT 24

For the filling

1 POUND RED OR PURPLE PLUMS, QUARTERED

⅓ CUP GRANULATED SUGAR

FINELY GRATED ZEST AND JUICE OF ½ ORANGE

For the dough

2½ CUPS ALL-PURPOSE FLOUR, PLUS EXTRA FOR DUSTING

¼ CUP GRANULATED SUGAR

¼ TEASPOON BAKING SODA

A GOOD PINCH OF GROUND CINNAMON

A PINCH OF SALT

FINELY GRATED ZEST OF ½ LEMON

¼ CUP MARSALA

4 TABLESPOONS UNSALTED BUTTER, MELTED AND SLIGHTLY COOLED

1 LARGE EGG, SEPARATED

4 CUPS SUNFLOWER OIL

CONFECTIONERS' SUGAR, FOR DUSTING

Equipment

PASTA MACHINE

4 TO 5-INCH PLAIN COOKIE CUTTER

SUGAR THERMOMETER

Start by making the filling: Place the plums, sugar, and orange zest and juice in a saucepan and cook over medium heat, stirring frequently, for about 30 minutes until the plums have cooked down to a jammy consistency. Keep a close eye on the mixture during the last moments of cooking and stir regularly to prevent it from sticking and burning on the bottom of the pan. Transfer into a bowl and let cool.

For the dough, sift the flour, granulated sugar, baking soda, cinnamon, and salt into a mixing bowl. Make a well in the middle and add the lemon zest, Marsala,

melted butter, and egg yolk. Mix well, adding a drop of water if needed to bring the dough together, but not too much, as it should be quite a dry dough. Knead for a couple of minutes until almost smooth. Cover with an upturned bowl or plastic wrap and let rest for 20 minutes.

Set up the pasta machine at one end of a work surface and lightly dust with flour. Divide the dough into thirds—this makes it easier to work with. Roll one piece into a rectangle ¼-inch thick, keeping the remaining pieces covered. Pass through the pasta machine on the widest setting. Fold in half and pass through again, then repeat. Reduce the thickness of the rollers by one notch and pass the dough through again. Repeat, rolling at increasingly thinner increments, until the dough is 1/16-inch thick—this is the last-but-one notch on my machine—keeping the work surface and your dough very lightly dusted with flour to prevent it from sticking.

Lay the rolled-out dough across the work surface, being careful not to stretch it. Using the cutter, stamp out discs from the dough. Gather up the offcuts into a ball and set aside. Spoon slightly less than a teaspoonful of plum compote into the middle of each disc, leaving a ¼-inch border all around. Brush one side of the exposed dough with a little of the reserved, lightly beaten egg white, fold the dough over the compote to make a crescent shape, and press the edges together to seal. Repeat with the remaining dough and compote. Any leftover dough can be thinly rolled, cut into strips, deep-fried, and dusted with confectioners' sugar.

Meanwhile, pour the oil into a large saucepan and set over medium heat. Pop the thermometer into the pan and bring the oil up to 325 to 350°F.

Cook the ravioli in batches of around six in the hot oil for about 3 minutes until golden, ensuring that the oil returns to the correct temperature before cooking the next batch. Remove with a slotted spoon, drain well on paper towels, and serve just warm, dusted with confectioners' sugar.

Roasted Plum Soufflés

Soufflés strike fear into the heart of many cooks, but these little delights are very easy to make, requiring only a thick plum purée enriched with egg yolks and a mound of pillowy sweetened egg whites. They rise beautifully and are light yet fruity, making them perfect to serve at the end of a rich meal. The plum purée can be prepared in advance and the soufflés cooked just before serving.

MAKES 6

1 QUANTITY OF ROASTED PLUMS
(SEE PAGE 128)

1 TEASPOON CORNSTARCH

1 TEASPOON LEMON JUICE (OPTIONAL)

MELTED UNSALTED BUTTER, FOR GREASING

⅓ CUP GRANULATED SUGAR, PLUS EXTRA FOR
DUSTING

2 MEDIUM EGG YOLKS

4 MEDIUM EGG WHITES

A PINCH OF CREAM OF TARTAR

A PINCH OF SALT

THICK CREAM, TO SERVE

Equipment

FINE-MESH NYLON SIEVE

6 × 5-FLUID OUNCE RAMEKINS

Once the plums have roasted, let them cool, then scoop all the fruit and juice into a bowl, picking out and discarding the pits, vanilla bean pieces, and cinnamon stick, and blend until smooth using an immersion blender or food processor. If you want a silky smooth sorbet, pass through a fine-mesh nylon sieve. This should yield 2 to 2¼ cups purée. Place in a saucepan over medium heat and cook gently, stirring frequently, for about 5 minutes until reduced to 1¾ cups. Mix the cornstarch with a teaspoon of cold water, stir into the purée, and simmer for another 30 seconds to thicken further and cook out the cornstarch. Taste and add the lemon juice if it needs sharpening, remembering you will be adding sugar later. Let cool slightly.

Preheat the oven to 375°F. Brush the inside of the ramekins neatly and smoothly with the melted butter, then dust with an even coating of granulated sugar and tap out any excess. Spoon a rounded teaspoonful of plum purée into the base of each ramekin and spread level. Beat the egg yolks into the remaining plum purée.

In a large mixing bowl, whisk the egg whites with the cream of tartar and salt until they will hold soft, floppy peaks. Gradually add the granulated sugar and whisk again until smooth and glossy.

Fold a large tablespoonful of the egg whites into the plum and egg yolk mixture to lighten it and then, using a large metal spoon, fold the purée back into the egg whites, being careful not to knock out the air. Spoon into the ramekins, slightly overfilling them and ensuring that the mixture fills them evenly without large air pockets. Using a palette knife, slice the excess mixture off the top of the soufflés level with the top of the ramekin. Run the tip of your thumb around the inside top edge of each ramekin and arrange on a solid baking sheet.

Slide onto the middle rack of the oven and bake for 10 minutes until well-risen, golden brown on top, and with a very slight wobble. Using a metal spatula, carefully and quickly transfer the ramekins to small plates and serve immediately with thick cream.

Crispy Duck with Spiced Plum Sauce

This plum sauce works perfectly as a dipping sauce for spring rolls and the like. The duck is also good with an Asian-style coleslaw and scallion or chive pancakes. Make this the day before serving as the duck will need to marinate in the fridge overnight.

SERVES 4; MAKES 2 JARS

For the duck

1 ROUNDED TEASPOON SICHUAN PEPPERCORNS

2 GARLIC CLOVES, COARSELY CHOPPED

2-INCH PIECE OF FRESH GINGER, CHOPPED

1 ROUNDED TEASPOON CHINESE FIVE-SPICE

4 DUCK LEGS

2 TABLESPOONS SOY SAUCE

1 TABLESPOON CHINESE BLACK RICE VINEGAR

For the plum sauce

1¼ POUNDS RED OR PURPLE PLUMS, COARSELY CHOPPED

1 SMALL RED ONION, CHOPPED

1 LARGE GARLIC CLOVE, CHOPPED

2-INCH PIECE OF FRESH GINGER, CHOPPED

1 RED CHILE, SEEDED AND CHOPPED

1 TEASPOON SICHUAN PEPPERCORNS

1 SMALL CINNAMON STICK

3 ALLSPICE BERRIES

1 TO 2 STAR ANISE

⅔ CUP LIGHT BROWN SUGAR

⅔ CUP CHINESE BLACK RICE VINEGAR

SOY SAUCE, TO TASTE (OPTIONAL)

SQUEEZE OF LIME JUICE, TO TASTE

To serve

PANCAKES

SHREDDED SCALLIONS AND CUCUMBER

Equipment

FINE-MESH NYLON SIEVE OR MOULIN A LEGUMES

2 × 12-OUNCE PRESERVING JARS

Start by preparing the duck: Put the Sichuan peppercorns in a small dry frying pan and toast over low to medium heat for a couple of minutes until they begin to smell aromatic. Grind using a mortar and pestle. Add the garlic and ginger to the mortar along with the five-spice and pound until almost smooth.

Lay the duck legs on a large platter and slash the skin on each leg a couple of times. Drizzle with the soy sauce and vinegar, rubbing it into both the meat and skin side of each leg. Using your hands, massage the spice mix into each leg to coat as evenly as possible. Cover with plastic wrap and chill in the fridge overnight.

To make the plum sauce, place the plums, onion, garlic, ginger, and chile in a large stainless steel saucepan. Pop the spices into the pan, add the sugar and vinegar, and mix to combine. Place the pan over low to medium heat and bring to a boil, stirring frequently to dissolve the sugar. Cook steadily for about 40 minutes, stirring from time to time, until the fruit is very tender and the mixture thickened.

Either push the mixture through a fine-mesh nylon sieve or a *moulin à légumes* to remove the spices and plum skins. Quickly wash the pan, return the strained sauce to it, and cook for another 3 to 4 minutes until thickened to the consistency of tomato ketchup. Taste the sauce and add a dash of soy sauce if it needs saltiness and a drop of freshly squeezed lime juice to sharpen it.

Spoon into a jar or bowl and leave until cold, then spoon into a sterilized mason or other preserving jar (see page 132), seal, and store in the fridge until needed. It will keep well for up to 6 weeks.

The next day, preheat the oven to 375°F. Pat the duck legs dry, rubbing off as much of the marinade as possible, arrange in a roasting pan, and cook in the oven for 25 to 30 minutes until the skin is crisp and the meat tender.

Shred the duck and serve Peking style with the plum sauce, along with pancakes and shredded scallions and cucumber.

Roasted Plums with Rice Pudding

Plums are enormously versatile and roasting them in this super-simple fashion will expand their uses even further. Although divine dished up just as they are or with a good puddle of cream, they are sublime served alongside rice pudding, as here, or when turned into a sorbet, soufflé, or unctuous cheesecake. Try them with your breakfast yogurt and granola or with a hot bowl of oatmeal—the list goes on…

I always recommend that you use ripe fruit for most recipes, but roasting slightly underripe plums will enhance any that are slightly lacking in the flavor department.

SERVES 6

For the roasted plums

1¾ POUNDS RIPE RED PLUMS, WASHED

1½ TABLESPOONS GRANULATED SUGAR

½ VANILLA BEAN

1 SMALL CINNAMON STICK

For the rice pudding

⅔ CUP SHORT-GRAIN RICE

1 VANILLA BEAN, SPLIT IN HALF LENGTHWISE

¼ TO ⅓ CUP GRANULATED SUGAR

1 STRIP OF ORANGE PEEL

2 GREEN CARDAMOM PODS, LIGHTLY CRUSHED

3 CUPS 1% MILK

A PINCH OF SALT

2 TO 3 TABLESPOONS HEAVY CREAM, PLUS EXTRA TO SERVE

1 TABLESPOON CHOPPED PISTACHIOS, ALMONDS, OR HAZELNUTS

Preheat the oven to 350°F and line a baking pan with parchment paper or foil.

For the roasted plums, cut the fruits in half—don't worry about removing the pits at this stage. Arrange in the lined pan, cut-side up, and sprinkle with the sugar. Split the half vanilla bean in half down its length and cut each piece in half again. Tuck the vanilla pieces and cinnamon stick among the plums and roast on the middle rack of the oven for 30 to 40 minutes until the fruit is very tender, juicy, and starting to caramelize at the edges.

Meanwhile, make the rice pudding: Place the rice in a saucepan, add 1½ cups cold water, and bring to a boil. Reduce the heat and simmer for 4 to 5 minutes. Drain and return to the pan.

Add the vanilla bean to the rice with ¼ cup sugar, the strip of orange peel, cardamom pods, milk, and salt. Place over low heat and bring slowly to a boil. Simmer very gently, stirring from time to time, for about 20 minutes until the rice is tender and most of the milk has been absorbed.

Remove from the heat, fish out the vanilla bean and orange peel, and add the cream and the rest of the sugar, if needed. Serve warm, scattered with the nuts, with the roasted plums and extra cream.

Roasted Plum Sorbet

My sister and I meet for a "light" supper in Soho about once a month and the evening generally follows the same pattern each time. We aim to eat somewhere vaguely healthy—as we're more often than not pretending to be watching what we eat—and then we amble through the streets of Central London to our favorite gelato bar and undo all the good we did earlier. This recipe is inspired by a sorbet that I had on one such evening in late summer, the scoops piled high into a waffle cone and dripping sticky-sweet plum juices down my hands—the perfect end to an evening.

SERVES 6 TO 8

1 QUANTITY OF ROASTED PLUMS
(SEE PAGE 128)

¾ CUP GRANULATED SUGAR

Equipment

FINE-MESH NYLON SIEVE (OPTIONAL)

ICE-CREAM MAKER

Once the plums have roasted, let them cool, then scoop all the fruit and juice into a bowl, picking out and discarding the pits, vanilla bean pieces, and cinnamon stick as you do so. Blend the plums until smooth—I find this easiest using an immersion blender, but otherwise transfer to a food processor—and then pass through a fine-mesh nylon sieve if you want a silky smooth sorbet. I don't mind the odd speckle of plum skin in the sorbet but it's down to personal preference.

Pour ¼ cup cold water into a saucepan and add the granulated sugar. Bring to a boil over medium heat, stirring to dissolve the sugar. Simmer for 2 minutes, then remove from the heat and add the roasted plum purée. Let cool, then cover and chill in the fridge for a couple of hours before churning in the ice-cream maker according to the manufacturer's instructions.

An ice-cream maker will make a lighter sorbet, but if you don't have one, simply freeze the mixture in a plastic freezer-safe container, whisking it every couple of hours to break up the ice crystals. Once the sorbet has frozen, break it into manageable chunks, transfer into a food processor, and blend until smooth and light. Return to the freezer container and freeze until firm.

Plum and Star Anise Jam

I like jam to be soft-set—I don't want to be able to stand my spoon up in the jar, but for the jam to dribble off my toast and onto my fingers so that I get in a sticky, fruity mess and have to add more. With that in mind, I err on the side of less sugar to fruit, which allows the fruitiness to shine through, although it does require perfectly ripe, juicy fruit.

MAKES 4 TO 5 JARS

3½ POUNDS RIPE PLUMS, WASHED

4 CUPS GRANULATED OR JAM SUGAR

1 CINNAMON STICK

2 STAR ANISE

Equipment

4 TO 5 × 16-OUNCE CANNING JARS

STAINLESS STEEL PRESERVING PAN

JAM FUNNEL (OPTIONAL)

Cut the plums into quarters, remove the pits, and put in a large glass or ceramic bowl. Add the sugar and stir well to thoroughly combine. Add the cinnamon stick and star anise and stir again. Cover with plastic wrap and leave at room temperature for 6 to 8 hours or overnight to allow the sugar to start to dissolve in the fruit juices.

Scoop the contents of the bowl into the preserving pan and set over low heat to dissolve any remaining sugar. Increase the heat to medium and bring to a boil, removing any foam that rises to the surface with a slotted spoon. Cook for about 20 minutes at a steady boil until the jam just reaches setting point. To test for setting point, drop a scant teaspoon of jam onto a chilled saucer, leave it for 30 seconds, and then push it with the tip of your finger. If the jam forms a light skin and wrinkles, it's ready; if not, continue to cook and test every couple of minutes until setting point has been reached.

Once setting point has been reached, remove the pan from the heat and let relax for 5 minutes—this will allow any larger fruit pieces to remain suspended in the jam once it is bottled rather than rising to the top of the jar.

Pick out the cinnamon stick and star anise, ladle the jam into a pitcher, and pour into the warm sterilized jars—using a jam funnel will make this an easier task—leaving ¼ to ½ inch headspace. Using a clean, damp paper towel, wipe the edges of the jars to remove any drips, screw the lids on tightly, and process in a water bath (see page 40). Leave until completely cold before labeling and storing in a cool, dark cupboard for up to 6 months and up to 2 months in the fridge after opening.

To sterilize canning jars, put them right-side-up on the rack in a boiling-water canner. Fill the canner and jars with hot (not boiling) water to 1-inch above the tops of the jars and boil for 10 minutes. Pop two saucers into the fridge or freezer ready for testing the jam for setting point.

White Peach and Raspberry Jam

Peaches and raspberries are a wonderful combination, particularly in this jam. Although raspberry jam is delicious, it can be heavy on the seeds, so my solution is to combine the berries with other fruits. If you can find white peaches, do use them here—the color is quite divine. You could also add the seeds scraped from a split vanilla bean if you like.

MAKES 4 TO 5 JARS

1¾ POUNDS OR 4 TO 5 LARGE WHITE-FLESHED PEACHES, WASHED

3¼ CUPS GRANULATED OR JAM SUGAR

JUICE OF 1 LEMON

12 OUNCES RASPBERRIES

Equipment

4 TO 5 × 16-OUNCE CANNING JARS

STAINLESS STEEL PRESERVING PAN

JAM FUNNEL (OPTIONAL)

Cut the peaches into wedges, removing the pits as you do so. Put the wedges in a large glass or ceramic bowl and add the sugar and lemon juice, stirring well to thoroughly combine. Cover with plastic wrap and leave at room temperature for 4 hours to allow the sugar to start to dissolve in the juices released from the peaches.

Sterilize the jars and chill two saucers to test for setting point, as for the Plum and Star Anise Jam (opposite). Scoop the sugary peaches into the preserving pan, add the raspberries, and then follow the method for the plum jam opposite from the second step to finish making the jam.

Apricot and Vanilla Jam

This jam in particular makes my case for majoring on fruitiness rather than sweetness. Adding the kernels from the apricot pits contributes a nutty, almondy note to the end result.

MAKES 4 TO 5 JARS

2½ POUNDS RIPE APRICOTS, WASHED

3¼ CUPS GRANULATED OR JAM SUGAR

JUICE OF 1 LEMON

1 VANILLA BEAN, SPLIT IN HALF LENGTHWISE

Equipment

4 TO 5 × 16-OUNCE CANNING JARS

STAINLESS STEEL PRESERVING PAN

JAM FUNNEL (OPTIONAL)

Cut the apricots into quarters, reserving the pits. Put in a large glass bowl and add the sugar and lemon juice. Mix well, cover, and leave at room temperature for 6 to 8 hours or overnight to allow the sugar to start to draw out and dissolve in the fruit juices. Meanwhile, take one apricot pit at a time, wrap in a clean kitchen towel, and bash with a rolling pin to crack the shell. Remove the kernel and set aside.

Sterilize the jars and chill two saucers to test for setting point, as for the Plum and Star Anise Jam (opposite). Bring a small saucepan of water to a boil, add the apricot kernels, and blanch for 1 to 2 minutes, then drain and set aside.

Scoop the contents of the bowl into the preserving pan, add the vanilla bean, and follow the method for the plum jam opposite from the second step to finish making the jam. When bottling, ensure that the apricot kernels are evenly divided between the jars.

Plum Streuselkuchen

This enriched dough has more in common with a cake than bread and is ideal to serve for a late breakfast, brunch, or mid-morning treat with a pot of steaming coffee. It's best eaten on the day of making but will reheat well if wrapped in foil and placed in a medium oven for a few minutes. You can prepare the dough the night before and let it rise in the fridge overnight before topping and baking. I like to use a mixture of plums for this cake, not only for flavor but for color too.

SERVES 8 TO 10

9 TABLESPOONS UNSALTED BUTTER, DICED AND SOFTENED, PLUS EXTRA FOR GREASING

½ CUP WHOLE MILK

2½ CUPS ALL-PURPOSE FLOUR

⅔ CUP GRANULATED SUGAR

½ TEASPOON GROUND CINNAMON

¼ OUNCE FAST-ACTION/EASY-BLEND DRIED YEAST

A GOOD PINCH OF SALT

⅓ CUP SOUR CREAM OR BUTTERMILK, AT ROOM TEMPERATURE

1 MEDIUM EGG

1 MEDIUM EGG YOLK

1 TEASPOON FINELY GRATED LEMON ZEST

1 TEASPOON VANILLA EXTRACT

1¼ POUNDS MIXED PLUMS, WASHED AND DRIED

For the streusel

¼ CUP LIGHT BROWN SUGAR

¼ CUP DARK BROWN SUGAR

A GOOD PINCH OF SALT

½ TEASPOON GROUND CINNAMON

⅔ CUP ALL-PURPOSE FLOUR

4 TABLESPOONS UNSALTED BUTTER, MELTED

Equipment

8-INCH SQUARE CAKE PAN

Grease the pan and line the bottom and sides with greased parchment paper.

Warm the milk until tepid—a shade hotter than body temperature. Put the flour in the bowl of a free-standing mixer fitted with a dough hook. Add the granulated sugar, cinnamon, yeast, and salt and mix with a balloon whisk to thoroughly combine. Make a well in the middle. Combine the sour cream or buttermilk, whole egg, yolk, lemon zest, and vanilla extract in a pitcher. Pour the warm milk into the mixer bowl, add the sour cream mixture and softened butter, and knead on medium speed for about 4 minutes until you have a silky smooth dough.

Scoop into the prepared pan and spread level using a palette knife. Cover loosely with plastic wrap and either let the dough rise slowly overnight in the fridge or for 2 to 3 hours at room temperature.

If you have left the dough overnight in the fridge, bring it to room temperature before proceeding to the next stage. Preheat the oven to 375°F.

Meanwhile, prepare the streusel: Mix the sugars, salt, cinnamon, and flour in a small bowl. Add the melted butter and stir well to combine—the mixture should start to form large clumps. Scatter one-third over the top of the cake. Cut the plums into quarters or sixths, depending on size, and arrange on top. Scatter the remaining streusel over the plums.

Bake the streuselkuchen on the middle rack of the oven for 20 minutes. Reduce the heat to 350°F and bake for another 45 to 50 minutes until the cake is well-risen, the streusel golden and crisp, the fruit tender, and a wooden skewer inserted into the middle of the cake comes out clean.

Damson Pâté de Fruit

Damsons—small, dark blue plums—are too bitter to be eaten raw but have a unique flavor once cooked and shown a little sugar. I like them just like that or tossed into a pie or crumble followed by the inevitable game of Tinker, Tailor, Soldier, Sailor. But they have a relatively short season, so are worth cooking with in as many ways as you can, and this is a valuable recipe to add to the repertoire. I love making *pâte de fruit* and am always looking for new fruits to give the pastille treatment to. The purée can be prepared and frozen in batches until ready to use, if you are like me and can't bear to be without your favorite fruits once the season is over.

MAKES ABOUT 40 PIECES

SUNFLOWER OIL, FOR OILING

1½ POUNDS DAMSON PLUMS, WASHED

1 TO 2 TABLESPOONS LEMON JUICE

2 CUPS GRANULATED SUGAR

½ OUNCE POWDERED PECTIN

¾ CUP GRANULATED SUGAR, FOR COATING

Equipment

FINE-MESH NYLON SIEVE

8-INCH SQUARE BAKING PAN

Lightly oil the baking pan and line the bottom and sides with plastic wrap, ensuring that it comes right up the sides of the pan.

Put the damsons in a saucepan that will accommodate them spaciously. Add the lemon juice and 2 to 3 tablespoons of the granulated sugar, cover, and cook over low heat, stirring from time to time, for about 20 minutes until the fruit has burst and become really soft and juicy. Transfer into a fine-mesh nylon sieve set over a bowl and push the fruit through until all that remains in the sieve is a little damson skin and the pits. Return the purée to the cleaned pan and reheat until boiling, then simmer for 2 minutes to thicken slightly.

In a bowl, whisk together the remaining granulated sugar and pectin—it needs to be thoroughly combined before adding to the purée. Add to the pan, stirring constantly with a wooden spoon or heatproof rubber spatula to dissolve the sugar. Simmer over medium heat, stirring frequently, until the mixture has thickened and a teaspoonful dropped into a small bowl of iced water immediately forms into a ball. Continue cooking and testing every couple of minutes until setting point has been reached.

Pour into the prepared pan and spread level. Leave in a cool place until completely cold and then cover with plastic wrap and leave until firm—preferably overnight.

The next day, spread the granulated sugar onto a baking sheet in an even layer. Carefully turn out the *pâte de fruit* onto the sugar, top-side down. Peel off the plastic wrap from the underside and, using a hot or lightly greased kitchen knife, cut into ½ to ¾-inch squares, coating each piece in the sugar as you do so to keep them from sticking together.

Leave the pastilles to dry for 30 minutes to 1 hour before shaking off the excess sugar and packaging into pretty boxes between layers of waxed or nonstick paper.

New York-style Cheesecake with Roasted Plums

This cheesecake is best made the day before serving, giving it plenty of time to cool, which will make slicing easier. The Roasted Plums are the perfect accompaniment, being fruity and sharp enough to cut through the creamy richness.

SERVES 8

1¾ CUPS GRAHAM CRACKERS, GINGERSNAPS, OR AMARETTI COOKIES

3 TABLESPOONS UNSALTED BUTTER, MELTED, PLUS EXTRA FOR GREASING

2½ CUPS FULL-FAT CREAM CHEESE

3 LARGE EGGS

1¼ CUPS SOUR CREAM

¾ CUP GRANULATED SUGAR

1 TABLESPOON CORNSTARCH

1 TEASPOON VANILLA EXTRACT

GRATED ZEST AND JUICE OF 1 LEMON

½ CUP GREEK-STYLE YOGURT

ROASTED PLUMS (SEE PAGE 128), TO SERVE

Equipment

8-INCH SPRINGFORM CAKE PAN

Preheat the oven to 350°F. Grease the pan and line the bottom with a disc of greased parchment paper.

Finely crush the graham crackers, either in a food processor or in a freezer bag using a rolling pin, and add to a bowl. Mix in the melted butter. Transfer into the prepared pan and press into an even layer over the bottom. Bake on the middle rack of the oven for 5 minutes.

Meanwhile, place the cream cheese, eggs, half the sour cream, ½ cup of the granulated sugar, and the cornstarch in a food processor and process until smooth. Scrape down the sides of the bowl with a rubber spatula and then add the vanilla extract and lemon zest and juice and process again.

Remove the pan from the oven and carefully pour the mixture over the graham cracker base. Place on a solid baking sheet and bake on the middle rack of the oven for about 35 minutes or until just set. Remove from the oven and let the cheesecake rest for 10 minutes, leaving the oven on.

Beat together the remaining sour cream, the yogurt, and remaining ¼ cup of granulated sugar. Carefully spoon this mixture on top of the cheesecake and return to the oven for another 10 minutes until set but not colored. Let the cheesecake cool completely before chilling.

Serve the cheesecake in slices with the Roasted Plums and their syrupy juices.

Vanilla and Thyme Baked Apricots

The fresh apricot season seems to come and go in a flash, so make the most of them while they're around. More often than not, the ones you see in the store are underripe and disappointing when eaten raw. They fare much better when shown a little heat, a little love, and something sweet to bring out their flavor and juiciness. This is the simplest and most delicious way of doing so, and even less-than-impressive apricots come alive when baked. Serve warm rather than hot, with the juices poured over and with a good slug of thick heavy cream. Or save for breakfast and top with natural yogurt and granola—preferably homemade, of course. It's one of those recipes where you don't need to be too specific—add a little more honey if you prefer and maybe a cinnamon stick, or even a handful of lightly toasted sliced almonds or pine nuts for crunch.

SERVES 3 TO 4

10 TO 12 RIPE APRICOTS

4 STRIPS OF LEMON PEEL

JUICE OF ½ LEMON

1 VANILLA BEAN

3 SPRIGS OF THYME

2 TO 3 TABLESPOONS HONEY

CHILLED HEAVY CREAM, TO SERVE

Preheat the oven to 375°F.

Wash the apricots and pat dry. Cut in half, remove the pits, and arrange the fruit, cut-side up, in a single layer in a ceramic ovenproof dish. Tuck the strips of lemon peel in among the fruit and drizzle with the lemon juice. Using the tip of a knife, slice the vanilla bean in half down its length and nestle both halves and the thyme sprigs around the apricots. Finally, drizzle with the honey and 2 tablespoons of cold water.

Bake on the middle rack of the oven for 20 to 25 minutes until tender, basting the apricots with the resulting juices halfway through cooking. The cooking timings can vary depending on the size and ripeness of the apricots, so keep an eye on them after 20 minutes, as you want the fruit to still hold its shape without becoming overly soft and mushy.

Serve warm with cold heavy cream.

Apricot and Vanilla Tart

Apricots nestled in a rich custard and baked inside a crisp, almondy crust—this is high summer in a tart and perfect for a lunch or dinner in the garden. When the fruits are not in peak condition, I suggest cooking with them to bring out their good side and this tart is sure to do just that. It's best served on the day of making, perhaps decorated with fresh lavender, and with extra crème fraîche, or vanilla ice cream if you're feeling indulgent—not that it needs it of course!

SERVES 8

For the dough

1¼ CUPS ALL-PURPOSE FLOUR, PLUS EXTRA
FOR DUSTING

¾ CUP GROUND ALMONDS

¼ CUP GRANULATED SUGAR

9 TABLESPOONS UNSALTED BUTTER,
CHILLED AND DICED

A GOOD PINCH OF SEA SALT

½ TABLESPOON ICED WATER

1 TEASPOON LEMON JUICE OR CIDER VINEGAR

1 MEDIUM EGG YOLK, LIGHTLY BEATEN

For the filling

1¾ TO 2¼ POUNDS APRICOTS, WASHED,
DRIED, HALVED, AND PITTED

1 VANILLA BEAN OR 1 TEASPOON VANILLA
BEAN PASTE

1 CUP CRÈME FRAÎCHE

1 MEDIUM EGG

2 MEDIUM EGG YOLKS

⅔ CUP GRANULATED SUGAR

½ CUP SLICED ALMONDS

CONFECTIONERS' SUGAR, TO DECORATE

Equipment

8½-INCH FLUTED TART PAN,
1½ INCHES DEEP

Start by making the dough. In a food processor, pulse together the flour, ground almonds, sugar, butter, and salt until there are only a very few small streaks of butter visible. Transfer to a bowl and make a well in the center. Mix the water with the lemon juice or vinegar and add to the bowl with the egg yolk. Bring the dough together using a palette knife and then, using your hands, gather the dough into a ball, being careful not to overwork it. Flatten into a disc, wrap in plastic wrap, and chill for a good couple of hours until firm.

Dust the work surface with flour and roll out the dough into a disc at least 1½ inches larger all around than the tart pan. Carefully roll the dough up around the rolling pin and unroll into the pan, ensuring that it is centrally positioned. Press the dough into the corners and flutes of the pan and trim off any excess from the top using a sharp knife. Prick the bottom with a fork and chill for 20 minutes while you prepare the filling and preheat the oven to 375°F. Place a solid baking sheet on the middle rack of the oven.

Arrange the apricot halves cut-side up in tight concentric circles, each slightly overlapping, in the tart crust. If using, split the vanilla bean in half down its length with a small sharp knife and scrape the seeds into a bowl, or add the vanilla bean paste. Add the crème fraîche, whole egg, yolks, and granulated sugar and whisk until smooth. Slowly pour the custard around the apricots, scatter with the sliced almonds, and slide the tart onto the hot baking sheet. Bake for about 1 hour until the crust is golden brown, the custard puffed and set, and the apricots starting to brown at the edges. You may need to turn the tart around halfway through to ensure that it cooks evenly.

Let cool to room temperature and serve with a light dusting of confectioners' sugar.

Peach and Buffalo Mozzarella Salad with Pistachio Pesto

I have rather romantic notions of making this salad after a leisurely stroll around an Italian market, carefully selecting the ripest peaches, most peppery arugula, and most beautiful tomatoes. As with all simple salads, success lies in using the absolute best, most flavorful produce you can find, so save this for high summer when the peaches are juicy and the tomatoes have been warmed by the sun. Failing that, get yourself to Italy and join me for a market wander. You can make it with burrata if you prefer, but it can be a little too creamy for my taste.

SERVES 4

For the pistachio pesto

½ CUP SHELLED UNSALTED PISTACHIOS, LIGHTLY TOASTED

1 GARLIC CLOVE, PEELED

½ CUP FLAT-LEAF PARSLEY

A DASH OF LEMON JUICE

½ CUP EXTRA VIRGIN OR PISTACHIO OIL

SALT AND FRESHLY GROUND BLACK PEPPER

4 RIPE PEACHES, WASHED AND DRIED

1 LEBANESE CUCUMBER OR ½ REGULAR CUCUMBER

6 HEIRLOOM TOMATOES, PREFERABLY MIXED COLORS

A GOOD HANDFUL OF ARUGULA

2 × 5-OUNCE BALLS BUFFALO MOZZARELLA

A HANDFUL OF PURPLE BASIL

3 TABLESPOONS AGED BALSAMIC VINEGAR

3 TABLESPOONS EXTRA VIRGIN OLIVE OIL

FRESHLY GROUND BLACK PEPPER

First make the pesto: Put the lightly toasted pistachios into the bowl of a mini processor and process until finely chopped. Add the garlic and parsley and process again to combine. Then add the lemon juice and half of the oil, season well with salt and black pepper, and blend until almost smooth. Add the remaining oil and process once more. Set aside for 30 minutes for all of the flavors to mingle, after which time taste the pesto and add more salt and pepper as needed.

Cut the peaches in half, remove the pits, and cut the fruit into wedges. Cut the cucumber into bite-sized pieces and slice the tomatoes. Arrange the arugula on each plate and top with peaches, cucumber, and tomatoes. Tear the mozzarella into pieces and divide between the plates. Spoon the pesto over each salad and scatter with the basil. Finish with a drizzle of the balsamic vinegar and extra virgin olive oil and a good grinding of black pepper.

Peach Shrub

Shrub is the name given to either a vinegared fruit syrup or to alcohol, often rum or brandy, that has fruit steeped in it. For this recipe we're sticking with the former. Don't turn the page yet, though, dismissing the notion of vinegared fruit syrup as the ramblings of a mad woman. When I was playing around with this recipe, most people I asked to taste test for me were skeptical at first. But what they discovered was a remarkably clean-tasting cordial—the vinegar is there but as an acidic back note to the vibrant peachy syrup.

Vinegar shrubs date from colonial America and were traditionally a way of preserving soft fruits, the vinegar acting as a preservative. They fell out of favor when commercially made cordials became widely available and with the advent of home refrigeration. Shrubs are now experiencing something of a renaissance and are deliciously refreshing when diluted with soda water and served with a good handful of ice or added to cocktails—try mixing with a measure of good-quality bourbon, vodka, or gin, topped with ginger ale, tonic water, or soda water.

MAKES 1 LARGE BOTTLE

6 RIPE YELLOW-FLESHED PEACHES, WASHED

1¾ CUPS GRANULATED SUGAR

1¼ CUPS WHITE BALSAMIC VINEGAR

Equipment

LARGE MASON OR OTHER PRESERVING JAR

FINE-MESH NYLON SIEVE

PIECE OF CLEAN CHEESECLOTH

16-OUNCE BOTTLE WITH CAP

Cut the peaches in half and remove the pits. Slice the fruit directly into a ceramic mixing bowl or large mason or other preserving jar. Add the sugar and mix to combine. Cover and pop in the fridge for 2 days, stirring twice a day until the fruit is super-soft and very juicy. You'll be amazed at how much juice is released from the fruit.

Add the vinegar, stir well, cover, and return to the fridge for another day, again stirring twice a day.

Pour the whole thing through a fine-mesh nylon sieve into a bowl and leave for a couple of hours to ensure that every last drop of juice drips through into the bowl. Don't be tempted to push the fruit, otherwise you'll end up with a cloudy pulp rather than clear syrup. Finally, pass the resulting liquid through clean cheesecloth before decanting into a sterilized bottle (see page 132). The shrub will keep for up to 1 month in the fridge.

When making shrub, it is of the utmost importance that you use ripe fruit, as you need to extract maximum flavor from the fruit and anything underripe won't have the necessary oomph and juice. If I happen to have a mixture of peaches in the fruit bowl—flat, white, or yellow-fleshed—I toss them all in together, sometimes adding a handful of raspberries or a couple of slices of fresh ginger for extra zing. The type of vinegar used plays an important part here too. I tried variations with cider vinegar and good-quality white wine vinegar but discovered that I much prefer using white balsamic. It has a more rounded, less acidic, less vinegary hit and is now widely available in larger supermarkets or in good delis.

Peach and Caramelized Honey Zabaglione Ice Cream with Pistachio Tuiles

Zabaglione is one of my all-time favorite desserts, whether served over sugared and sliced strawberries or peaches—the combination of eggs, sugar, and Marsala whisked over heat to produce pale clouds of deliciousness is quite dreamy. I also like zabaglione cooled and folded into softly whipped cream. And I like ice cream and peaches. So I've put all of those things together here. For the purists out there, I am aware that this is not strictly zabaglione, but this ice cream does at least have all the necessary elements—with a few added extras. The honey gives the ice cream a slightly softer set while enhancing the peachiness of the fruit. For best results, your peaches must be ripe and juicy—not only will underripe fruit be tricky to peel, but the flavor will be somewhat less fabulous. As the ice cream recipe uses only egg yolks, I've included a recipe for Pistachio Tuiles that will at least go some way to using up the egg whites and provide you with something crunchy to serve with the ice cream. They are best eaten on the day of making, but can be kept in an airtight container for another day and crisped up in a medium oven.

SERVES 6

For the ice cream

4 LARGE, RIPE YELLOW-FLESHED PEACHES

⅓ CUP FRAGRANT HONEY

JUICE OF ½ LEMON

¾ CUP WHOLE MILK

1¼ CUPS HEAVY CREAM

½ VANILLA BEAN, SPLIT IN HALF LENGTHWISE

4 MEDIUM EGG YOLKS

⅓ CUP GRANULATED SUGAR

2 TO 3 TABLESPOONS MARSALA

A SMALL PINCH OF SALT

For the pistachio tuiles

½ CUP SHELLED UNSALTED PISTACHIOS

⅔ CUP GRANULATED SUGAR

½ CUP ALL-PURPOSE FLOUR

3 MEDIUM EGG WHITES

A PINCH OF SALT

½ TEASPOON VANILLA EXTRACT

5 TABLESPOONS UNSALTED BUTTER, MELTED AND SLIGHTLY COOLED

Equipment

ICE-CREAM MAKER

PLASTIC FREEZER-SAFE CONTAINER

Cut a small cross on the underside of each peach. Place in a bowl, cover with boiling water, and leave for 30 seconds. Drain and run cold water over to loosen the skins; they should now slide off easily with the aid of the knife. Cut the peaches into quarters, discarding the pits, and slice into wedges.

Bring the honey to a boil in a medium saucepan over low to medium heat, then cook gently until reduced by nearly half and starting to darken to an amber-colored caramel. Add the peaches and lemon juice, combine, and cook, stirring frequently, for 8 to 10 minutes until the peaches break down into a pulp. Using an immersion blender or food processor, blend the mixture until smooth.

Pour the milk and half the cream into a medium, heavy-bottomed pan. Add the split vanilla bean, bring slowly to a boil, and then immediately remove from the heat and let infuse for 10 minutes.

Using a hand-held mixer, beat the egg yolks with the sugar in a bowl until really pale and light. Add the Marsala and salt and beat to combine. Reheat the milk, then pour onto the egg yolk mixture and whisk constantly until smooth. Return to the pan and heat gently, stirring constantly, until thick enough to coat the back of a wooden spoon—don't let it boil or you might scramble the eggs.

Remove from the heat, add the remaining cream and the peach purée, and whisk to combine. Strain into a clean bowl and leave until completely cold. Cover and chill for at least 2 hours but preferably overnight, then churn in the ice-cream maker according to the manufacturer's instructions. Scoop into a plastic freezer-safe container and freeze until needed.

For the tuiles, finely chop the pistachios in a food processor—you still want visible nutty pieces. Add the sugar and flour and process again until combined.

Whisk the egg whites with the salt in a bowl until they hold soft, floppy peaks. Add the vanilla and whisk to combine. Fold in the dry ingredients using a large metal spoon. Pour the melted butter around the sides of the bowl and fold in until thoroughly combined. Cover with plastic wrap and chill for 1 hour.

Preheat the oven to 300°F and line 2 baking sheets with parchment paper. Drop 4 heaping teaspoonfuls of mixture onto each sheet and spread each into thin 4 to 5-inch discs. Bake on the middle rack for 10 to 12 minutes until starting to turn golden brown at the edges. Working quickly, slide a palette knife under each tuile, lift off the pan, and either wrap around a wooden spoon handle or drape over a rolling pin. They will harden very quickly, which is why you bake only a few at a time. Repeat until all the batter has been used up.

Poached Peaches with Vanilla and Lemon Verbena

You can use either white- or yellow-fleshed peaches for this recipe, but I do love the rather elegant subtle hues of the white variety. Add a handful of fresh raspberries or redcurrants to the peaches after poaching for a pop of color and contrast.

SERVES 6

½ CUP GRANULATED SUGAR

2 STRIPS OF PEEL FROM A LEMON

2 STRIPS OF ORANGE PEEL

JUICE OF ½ LEMON

2 CUPS SWEET WINE, SUCH AS MUSCAT OR
LILLET ROSÉ

1 VANILLA BEAN, SPLIT IN HALF LENGTHWISE

1 LARGE SPRIG OF LEMON VERBENA

6 RIPE PEACHES

A HANDFUL OF RASPBERRIES OR
REDCURRANTS (OPTIONAL)

To make the poaching syrup, place the sugar, lemon and orange peels, lemon juice, and sweet wine into a deep sauté pan. Add the vanilla bean with the lemon verbena and 2 cups cold water. Bring slowly to a boil to dissolve the sugar, then lower the heat to a very gentle simmer.

Meanwhile, prepare the peaches: Cut a small cross through the skin on the underside of each peach. Place in a large bowl, cover with boiling water, and leave for 30 seconds to 1 minute to loosen the skin, then drain and rinse under cold water. Carefully peel the peaches.

Gently lower the peaches into the simmering syrup, cover with a disc of parchment paper, and poach for about 15 minutes or until tender when tested with the tip of a small, sharp knife—the cooking time will vary depending on the ripeness of the fruit.

Using a slotted spoon, transfer the peaches to a bowl. Increase the heat under the poaching syrup and boil until reduced by one-third of its original volume. Strain and pour over the peaches, add a handful of raspberries or redcurrants if you like, and leave until cold.

Tropical

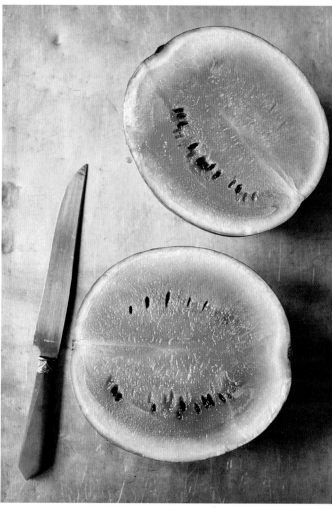

It was really tempting to throw the doors open wide with tropical fruit and include such delights as tamarillos and guavas, but instead I have attempted to stick to those fruits that are more readily available year round.

Most tropical fruits, with the exception of persimmons and melons, come from the southern hemisphere, as they require warmer climes and degrees of humidity. Persimmons also grow well in California, among other places, and melons in the more southern European countries.

Almost all tropical fruits protect their sweet delicate flesh with a thick and sometimes impenetrable skin—think coconuts and pineapples. This can make testing for ripeness tricky. When buying melons I always smell the underside of the fruit—it should smell sweet, aromatic, and "melony" if ripe and ready to eat. Probably the only time that I'll suggest using underripe fruit in a recipe is when making green papaya salad—a classic dish served throughout Southeast Asia in one guise or another. Green papayas are large underripe fruits often sold in the vegetable section of Asian supermarkets.

If you've ever traveled to the tropics then you have no doubt eaten fragrant, aromatic mangoes, bananas, and papayas—the like of which we rarely get to see in northern Europe or the US—as fruit is picked at its peak of ripeness and intended to be eaten fresh rather than being packed into crates and shipped around the world. India is one of the largest producers of mangoes in the world but only a very small percentage is exported. Luckily for us, fabulous mangoes are also grown from Brazil to Thailand. They vary hugely in size, color, and sweetness, with some of the best varieties having a bright egg-yolk yellow, silky smooth, almost buttery flesh.

Green Papaya Salad with Crispy Fried Beef

Green papayas, or pawpaws, are large, underripe papayas that are used as a vegetable in Thai or Vietnamese cooking and usually feature in versions of this refreshing salad. I wanted to add something extra to serve alongside, and found inspiration for the crispy fried beef from my local Vietnamese restaurant. It's substantial enough for a light lunch or can be served as an appetizer. Add halved cherry tomatoes and lightly blanched green beans for extra color and texture. Green papayas, Thai basil, and crispy fried shallots can all be found in good Asian food stores and markets. The recipe makes possibly more beef than you need, but it's not really worth the bother to make less. Any leftovers will keep for up to a week in an airtight container in the fridge and can be served with noodles or egg fried rice, or just as a snack.

SERVES 4

For the beef

18 OUNCES SKIRT STEAK, IN ONE PIECE

1 TABLESPOON DARK SOY SAUCE

2 TABLESPOONS LIGHT SOY SAUCE

1 ROUNDED TABLESPOON PALM OR LIGHT BROWN SUGAR

1 LEMONGRASS STALK, TRIMMED

2 GARLIC CLOVES, SLICED

1-INCH PIECE OF FRESH GINGER, SHREDDED

1 LARGE RED CHILE, SLICED

To finish

2 GARLIC CLOVES, COARSELY CHOPPED

1½-INCH PIECE OF FRESH GINGER, COARSELY CHOPPED

2 TEASPOONS PALM OR LIGHT BROWN SUGAR

1 TEASPOON GROUND CORIANDER

A GOOD PINCH OF GROUND CUMIN

¼ CUP COCONUT MILK

A PINCH OF SALT

2 TABLESPOONS SUNFLOWER OIL

4 TEASPOONS TAMARIND PASTE

SQUEEZE OF LIME JUICE

For the salad

1 MEDIUM GREEN PAPAYA

1 RED ONION, FINELY SLICED

A GOOD HANDFUL OF BEANSPROUTS, RINSED

1 GARLIC CLOVE, PEELED

2 RED BIRD'S EYE CHILES, COARSELY CHOPPED

1 LEMONGRASS STALK, TRIMMED AND SLICED

2 TO 3 TEASPOONS PALM OR LIGHT BROWN SUGAR

2 TO 3 TABLESPOONS FISH SAUCE, OR TO TASTE

JUICE OF 2 LIMES, OR TO TASTE

A HANDFUL OF THAI BASIL OR MINT, LEAVES TORN

A HANDFUL OF CILANTRO LEAVES

2 TABLESPOONS CRISPY ASIAN SHALLOTS (OPTIONAL)

2 TABLESPOONS COARSELY CHOPPED SALTED PEANUTS

Preheat the oven to 350°F.

Put the beef into a flameproof casserole with a tight-fitting lid. Mix together the soy sauces and sugar and pour over the beef. Bruise the lemongrass stalk with the back of a knife and cut in half, then add to the pan with the garlic, ginger, and chile and mix well with your hands. Add enough cold water to half cover the meat and slowly bring to a boil. Cover with the lid and cook in the oven for 1 hour or until the meat is very tender and will shred easily. Let cool in the broth, then drain and chill for a couple of hours or overnight.

Using your hands, pull the beef into long shreds and place in a large bowl. Using a mortar and pestle, pound the garlic and ginger with the sugar and spices until smooth. Add to the beef along with the coconut milk and salt. Mix, using clean hands, until thoroughly combined.

Heat the oil in a large frying pan, add the beef mixture, and fry over low to medium heat until dry and crisp, stirring frequently. This will take a good 20 minutes and

shouldn't be rushed. Add the tamarind paste and lime juice and cook for another minute. Let cool to room temperature while you prepare the salad.

Peel the papaya, cut in half, scoop out any seeds, then cut into fine matchsticks using a sharp knife or mandolin and add to a bowl. Add the red onion and beansprouts. Using the mortar and pestle, pound together the garlic,

chiles, lemongrass, and sugar until finely mashed and combined. Add the fish sauce and lime juice, taste, and add more sugar, fish sauce, or lime juice to balance the flavors. Pour over the salad, add the herbs, and mix to combine. Spoon onto serving plates, scatter with the crispy shallots, if using, and peanuts, and serve immediately with a generous helping of the beef.

Mango and Chile Hot Sauce

This sauce is great as a dip for potato wedges or fries and is also good served with barbecued sausages or burgers. In fact, I tend to use it whenever I would use ketchup. I have opted for the larger, medium-hot red chiles here, which I think give a good depth and balance of heat, but feel free to add a couple of bird's eye chiles if your chile tolerance levels are on the high side. But just remember that it's not big or clever to make a chile sauce that's too hot to eat, brings you or your guests out in a sweat, and renders you speechless.

MAKES 2 TO 3 JARS

14 OUNCES LARGE, MEDIUM-HOT RED CHILES

5 FAT GARLIC CLOVES, COARSELY CHOPPED

½ CUP FRESH GINGER, COARSELY CHOPPED

1 FAT OR 2 SLIM LEMONGRASS STALKS, TOUGH OUTER LEAVES DISCARDED, INNER STALKS TRIMMED AND SLICED

1 CUP CIDER OR RICE VINEGAR

1 TO 1⅓ CUPS LIGHT BROWN SUGAR

2 STAR ANISE

1 TEASPOON SEA SALT

4 LARGE RIPE MANGOES

2 TEASPOONS FISH SAUCE

JUICE OF 1 LIME

Equipment

2 TO 3 × 16-OUNCE CANNING JARS

Slice the stalk off each chile, then cut in half lengthwise and coarsely chop the flesh—don't remove the seeds. Add to the bowl of a food processor with the garlic, ginger, and lemongrass and pulse until finely chopped. Using a rubber spatula, scoop the mixture into a large, stainless steel saucepan. Wash the food processor bowl and blade immediately to prevent them becoming chile-tainted.

Add the vinegar, sugar, star anise, and salt to the pan and place over medium heat. Bring to a simmer, stirring frequently to dissolve the sugar, and cook for 5 to 10 minutes.

Meanwhile, slice off the cheeks—the rounded fleshy pieces either side of the thin pit—of each mango. Using the tip of the knife, cut a grid into the cut side of each mango cheek all the way down to (but not through) the skin. Push the mango cheek outward so that the skin is inverted and the flesh exposed in perfect little cubes. It's now easy to slice off all the flesh. Slice the skin away from the mango pit section and then carefully slice the mango flesh away from the pit. Add all the mango flesh to the pan with the fish sauce and lime juice, stir well, and continue to cook for about 40 minutes until very soft and the sauce starts to thicken to the consistency of ketchup. I find it helps to have the extractor fan on to keep the chile fumes to a minimum.

Slide the pan off the heat, let cool for a couple of minutes, and then blend the sauce until it's as smooth as possible, either in the food processor or a blender or using an immersion blender. Push the sauce through a fine-mesh nylon sieve and pour into the warm sterilized jars (see page 132), seal with the lids, and leave until cold before labeling and storing in the fridge. It will keep for up to 3 months.

Roasted Chile-spiked Pineapple

The first time I made this, I greedily ate almost the entire pineapple, with my fingers, standing up, and moments after pulling it out of the oven. I could barely wait for it to cool—the intense aroma of pineapple was speaking to me. The sliced red chile gives the pineapple and its resulting syrup a warming glow without blowing your socks off. And the dark rum just rounds things off, but obviously leave it out if children are involved.

SERVES 4 TO 6

1 LARGE RIPE PINEAPPLE

1 LARGE MEDIUM-HOT RED CHILE, SLICED

2-INCH PIECE OF FRESH GINGER, SLICED

1 STAR ANISE

1 SMALL CINNAMON STICK

¼ CUP LIGHT BROWN SUGAR

A PINCH OF SEA SALT

JUICE OF 1 LARGE JUICY LIME

3 PASSION FRUIT, HALVED

2 TABLESPOONS DARK RUM (OPTIONAL)

This method of preparing a pineapple sounds tricky but is in fact brilliant. Pineapples are prepared in this way on street-side fruit stalls all over Southeast Asia and I was first shown it by Lizzie Mabbott, a fellow food writer with an amazing knowledge of Asian cooking. Now that I've mastered it, I'll never go back to trying to gouge out the prickly "eyes" from the pineapple with the tip of a knife.

Line a baking sheet with parchment paper or foil.

Slice the leafy top and the tough bottom stalk end off the pineapple so that you have a flat underside. Stand the pineapple on its flat bottom and, using a long, sharp knife, cut the skin in strips from the pineapple, working from top to bottom and using a sawing action. Now take a look at the pineapple and you'll notice that the fibrous "eyes" go around the pineapple in helter-skelter diagonal lines from top to bottom. Pick one of the eyes at the top of the pineapple as your starting point and, using a smaller sharp knife, make a neat wedge cut in a line diagonally down the pineapple on either side of the eyes, cutting them out neatly. Repeat with all the eyes. What you should end up with is a neat barrel-shaped pineapple with grooves running down the outside of the flesh in a corkscrew fashion.

Cut the pineapple in half through the core from top to bottom. Cut in half again to give even-sized quarters, then slice out the hard core from each quarter and cut each quarter in half again to make eight neat wedges. Arrange on the lined baking sheet. Add the chile, ginger, star anise, cinnamon stick, sugar, and salt. Mix gently with your hands to thoroughly coat and set aside for 20 to 30 minutes so that the sugar dissolves and the pineapple starts to release its juice. Meanwhile, preheat the oven to 400°F.

Slide the baking sheet into the hot oven and bake the pineapple for about 30 minutes until tender and golden at the edges. You may need to carefully turn the pineapple pieces over halfway through to ensure that they cook and start to caramelize evenly.

Remove from the oven and immediately pour over the lime juice. Scoop the seeds and juice from the passion fruit halves into the pan and add the rum, if using. Gently turn the pineapple over in the juices to coat thoroughly and let cool for 5 minutes before serving, preferably with Toasted Coconut Ice Cream (see page 168).

Hummingbird Cake

I never tire of saying it, but you really do need to use ripe fruit for this recipe. A pineapple that is super-sweet and juicy and bananas with skins that are mottled with brown spots will result in a moist and truly flavorful cake. Hummingbird cake hails from the South and is more often than not made using canned crushed pineapple, which you could use here at a pinch. Using fresh, though, gives you the perfect excuse to use the remaining pineapple half to make the candied pineapple wafers. You also have the option of using coconut crystals in place of brown sugar; both this and the coconut nectar (available from health-food stores and suppliers) have a warm, caramel flavor with just a hint of coconut, making them ideal for this recipe.

SERVES 8 TO 10

2¼ CUPS ALL-PURPOSE FLOUR

1 TEASPOON BAKING POWDER

1 TEASPOON BAKING SODA

1 TEASPOON GROUND CINNAMON

¼ TEASPOON PUMPKIN PIE SPICE

A PINCH OF SALT

⅔ CUP GRANULATED SUGAR

⅔ CUP COCONUT CRYSTALS OR
LIGHT BROWN SUGAR

9 OUNCES RIPE PINEAPPLE FLESH (PREPARED
WEIGHT—ABOUT ½ MEDIUM PINEAPPLE)

2 LARGE RIPE BANANAS

⅓ CUP COCONUT OIL OR UNSALTED BUTTER,
PLUS EXTRA BUTTER FOR GREASING

½ CUP SUNFLOWER OIL

3 MEDIUM EGGS, LIGHTLY BEATEN

1 TEASPOON VANILLA EXTRACT

⅔ CUP PECANS, CHOPPED

½ CUP SHREDDED COCONUT

For the pineapple wafers

¼ CUP GRANULATED SUGAR

JUICE OF ½ LIME

¾-INCH PIECE FRESH GINGER,
COARSELY CHOPPED

2 TABLESPOONS DARK RUM

2 TABLESPOONS WATER

½ MEDIUM RIPE PINEAPPLE

Preheat the oven to 350°F. Grease and line the bottom of each cake pan with a disc of greased parchment paper.

Sift the flour, baking powder, baking soda, spices, and salt into a large mixing bowl. Add the sugars and mix well to combine. Make a well in the middle and set aside.

Finely chop the pineapple and mash the bananas. Gently melt the coconut oil or butter in a small saucepan over low heat, or in the microwave on a low setting, and add the sunflower oil. Pour into the middle of the dry ingredients, add the eggs and vanilla, and beat until almost smooth. Add the pineapple, bananas, pecans, and shredded coconut and stir until smooth.

Divide the mixture evenly between the prepared cake pans and bake on the middle rack of the oven for 25 to 30 minutes or until well-risen, golden brown, and a skewer inserted into the middle of the cakes comes out clean. Let rest in the pans for 2 to 3 minutes and then carefully turn onto a wire rack to cool completely.

For the pineapple wafers, preheat the oven to 225°F. Cover a solid baking sheet with nonstick parchment paper.

Combine all the ingredients, except the pineapple, in a small saucepan and heat gently to dissolve the sugar. Bring to a boil and then simmer for 30 seconds. Remove from the heat.

Peel the pineapple and, using a long, sharp knife or a mandolin, slice into wafer-thin slices. Dip each slice into the rum syrup and arrange in a single layer on the lined baking sheet. Bake on the middle rack of the oven for around 1 hour until slightly golden and crisp, turning the slices over after 30 minutes and the pan around to ensure that they dry evenly. Lay the slices on a wire rack until cold and crisp.

For the frosting

18 OUNCES FULL-FAT CREAM CHEESE

2 TABLESPOONS COCONUT NECTAR
OR HONEY

¼ TEASPOON GROUND CINNAMON

1 CUP PECANS, FINELY CHOPPED

½ CUP COCONUT FLAKES

Equipment

3 × 8-INCH ROUND CAKE PANS

For the frosting, beat the cream cheese, nectar or honey, and cinnamon together in a bowl until smooth and thickened. Place one cake layer on a serving plate or cake stand and spread with 2 tablespoons of the frosting. Top with a second cake layer and more frosting. Carefully add the third cake and cover the top and sides with the remaining frosting, spreading it evenly and smoothly with a palette knife. Scatter the sides with the pecans and the top with the coconut flakes and pineapple wafers.

Mango and Passion Fruit Cake

This cake is a veritable ray of sunshine on a plate. Be sure to use juicy, ripe mangoes. They won't necessarily be as easy to slice as underripe fruit but will taste vastly superior. Try to arrange the slices as neatly as possible for a picture-perfect result.

SERVES 8

1½ CUPS GRANULATED SUGAR

16 TABLESPOONS (2 STICKS) UNSALTED BUTTER, SOFTENED, PLUS EXTRA FOR GREASING

1½ TEASPOONS VANILLA EXTRACT OR VANILLA BEAN PASTE

3 LARGE PASSION FRUIT, HALVED

2 LARGE OR 3 SMALL RIPE MANGOES

4 MEDIUM EGGS, LIGHTLY BEATEN

1¾ CUPS ALL-PURPOSE FLOUR

2 TEASPOONS BAKING POWDER

A PINCH OF FINE SEA SALT

2 TABLESPOONS SOUR CREAM, AT ROOM TEMPERATURE

Equipment

8-INCH ROUND HEAVY-BOTTOMED CAKE PAN

Preheat the oven to 350°F and grease the bottom and sides of the cake pan.

Heat ½ cup of the sugar with 2 tablespoons cold water in a small saucepan over low heat to dissolve the sugar. Bring to a boil and continue to cook without stirring until the sugar has turned an amber caramel color. Add 3 tablespoons of the butter and ½ teaspoon of the vanilla and swirl the pan to incorporate evenly. Immediately pour into the prepared cake pan, covering the bottom with an even layer of caramel, then let cool slightly. Scoop the seeds and juice from the halves of 1 passion fruit over the top of the caramel.

Peel the mangoes, slice off the "cheeks" on either side of the narrow pit, and thinly slice the flesh. Slice the remaining mango flesh from around the pit. Arrange the slices neatly, slightly overlapping, over the cold, hard caramel.

Using a free-standing mixer, cream the remaining butter and sugar together until pale, light, and fluffy. Gradually add the beaten eggs, mixing well between each addition and scraping down the sides of the bowl with a rubber spatula from time to time. Sift in the flour, baking powder, and salt, add the seeds and juice of the remaining 2 passion fruit and the sour cream, and mix again until smooth and thoroughly combined.

Carefully spoon the cake mixture over the mango slices and spread level using a palette knife or the back of the spoon. Bake on the middle rack of the oven for 50 minutes to 1 hour or until a skewer inserted into the middle of the cake comes out clean. If it's browning too quickly, reduce the oven temperature to 350°F or loosely cover the top of the cake with parchment paper. Let cool in the pan for 5 minutes before turning onto a serving dish.

Mango and Passion Fruit Sorbet

Something this easy and delicious is a winner in my book. If you can find Alphonso mangoes, which have a tender, juicy, and vibrant, almost egg yolk-orange flesh and an intense sweetness, then use them. You may want to increase the lime juice slightly if your mangoes are super-sweet—but just enough to balance the flavor. You could also add some freshly grated ginger or a tiny amount of fresh red chile for extra oomph. If you want to make the sorbet without an ice-cream maker, freeze the mixture in a plastic freezer-safe container for 2 hours, whisk it to break up the ice crystals, and repeat the freezing and whisking process another three times until the sorbet is firm. You could then blitz the sorbet in a food processor to lighten it further. Using an ice-cream maker, however, will result in a very light, almost creamy sorbet.

SERVES 8

3 MEDIUM OR 2 LARGE RIPE MANGOES

JUICE OF 1 LIME

3 LARGE PASSION FRUIT

1¼ CUPS GRANULATED SUGAR

A PINCH OF SALT

Equipment

ICE-CREAM MAKER (OR SEE RECIPE INTRODUCTION)

PLASTIC FREEZER-SAFE CONTAINER

Peel the mangoes and slice all the flesh into a blender and add the lime juice. Blend the fruit until silky smooth and pour into a bowl. Cut the passion fruit in half and scoop the juice and seeds into a sieve placed over the bowl. Push all the pulp and juice from the passion fruit into the mango purée and discard the seeds.

Put the sugar in a medium saucepan, add 1 cup cold water and the salt, and bring slowly to a boil to dissolve the sugar. Simmer for 2 minutes, then remove from the heat and let cool for 15 minutes before adding to the fruit. Stir until combined and leave until cold before thoroughly chilling in the fridge for at least 2 hours but preferably overnight.

Churn the mixture in an ice-cream maker according to the manufacturer's instructions. Transfer to a plastic freezer-safe container, cover, and freeze until firm before serving.

Toasted Coconut Ice Cream

This is perfect when served alongside the Roasted Chile-spiked Pineapple on page 163 or with Mango and Passion Fruit Sorbet, above, but is equally delicious when drizzled with a warm dark chocolate sauce.

SERVES 6 TO 8

½ CUP SHREDDED COCONUT

1 CUP WHOLE MILK

1 CUP COCONUT MILK

4 LARGE EGG YOLKS

¼ CUP COCONUT CRYSTALS AND ¼ CUP GRANULATED
SUGAR, OR ½ CUP GRANULATED SUGAR

1 TEASPOON VANILLA EXTRACT OR VANILLA BEAN PASTE

¾ CUP HEAVY CREAM

2 TABLESPOONS DARK RUM (OPTIONAL)

FRESHLY GRATED NUTMEG

Equipment

FINE-MESH NYLON SIEVE

ICE-CREAM MAKER

PLASTIC FREEZER-SAFE CONTAINER

Put the coconut in a frying pan and toast over low to medium heat until golden brown, shaking the pan regularly to prevent it from scorching. Transfer into a bowl and let cool.

Heat the milk and coconut milk in a saucepan over medium heat to just below boiling point. Meanwhile, whisk the egg yolks, sugar, and vanilla together in a bowl until very pale and thick. Add the hot milk mixture in a steady stream, whisking constantly until smooth. Return to the pan and cook over low heat, stirring constantly, until it thickens enough to coat the back of the spoon, but don't allow it to boil or the eggs may scramble. Strain through a fine-mesh nylon sieve into a clean bowl. Add the cream, rum, if using, and a good grating of nutmeg. Let cool completely, then chill thoroughly for a good couple of hours, preferably overnight.

Churn the mixture in an ice-cream maker according to the manufacturer's instructions. Stir in the toasted coconut, then spoon into a plastic freezer-safe container, cover, and freeze until required.

Pineapple Empanadas

This recipe for sweet empanadas uses the same cream cheese dough as my Apple Tarte Tatin on page 208. The buttery, flaky pastry is not only easy to make, but perfectly complements the sweet, slightly spiced pineapple filling. These empanadas are irresistible and are best eaten while still warm—as my editor Judith and photographer Tara will testify. Coconut or vanilla ice cream would be delicious served alongside.

MAKES ABOUT 16

For the filling

1 MEDIUM RIPE PINEAPPLE, PEELED, CORED, AND COARSELY CHOPPED

JUICE OF 1 LIME

2 TABLESPOONS LIGHT BROWN SUGAR

A GENEROUS PINCH OF ANCHO CHILE POWDER

1 TEASPOON GROUND CINNAMON

1 TABLESPOON GRANULATED SUGAR

2 TABLESPOONS MILK

For the empanadas

1 QUANTITY OF CREAM CHEESE PASTRY DOUGH (SEE PAGE 208), CHILLED

ALL-PURPOSE FLOUR, FOR DUSTING

Equipment

4½ TO 5-INCH PLAIN COOKIE CUTTER

Place the pineapple, lime juice, brown sugar, chile powder, and a good pinch of the cinnamon in a sauté pan and cook over low to medium heat until the fruit is tender, slightly sticky, and caramelized. Remove from the heat and let cool.

Preheat the oven to 350°F and line two baking sheets with parchment paper. In a small bowl, mix the remaining cinnamon with the granulated sugar.

Lightly dust the work surface with flour and roll out the chilled pastry dough to a thickness of ¹⁄₁₆-inch. Using the cutter, stamp out as many discs from the dough as you can, re-rolling the trimmings and stamping out more. Lay the discs out on the work surface and spoon 1 teaspoonful of the filling into the middle of each. Brush the edges with a little milk and fold the dough over the filling to make half-moon shapes, completely encasing the filling. Press the edges to seal and arrange on the lined baking sheets. Press the tines of a fork around the edges of each empanada, brush the tops with milk, and sprinkle with the cinnamon sugar.

Bake on the middle rack of the oven for about 20 minutes until golden brown and crisp.

Try swapping or upping the spices in the pineapple filling—a pinch of ground cardamom or aniseed would be quite lovely. As for the ancho chile powder, this is available in good delis or online and has a sweet, fruity smokiness to it rather than a head-popping chile heat.

Goat's Milk Labneh with Carrot, Beet, and Pomegranate Salad

Labneh is simply natural yogurt that has been seasoned and strained overnight through cheesecloth until it becomes like a soft cheese. I like to use goat's milk yogurt as it has a more grassy taste than regular yogurt which contrasts deliciously with the sweet, roasted carrots and beets and sharp pomegranate seeds. You could also add a crushed clove of garlic and a pinch of ground cumin seeds to pep up the labneh, and of course use regular yogurt if you prefer.

SERVES 4 TO 6

18 OUNCES FULL-FAT GOAT'S MILK YOGURT

SALT AND FRESHLY GROUND BLACK PEPPER

A BUNCH OF SMALL CARROTS

A BUNCH OF MIXED SMALL BEETS

3 TABLESPOONS OLIVE OIL

3 GARLIC CLOVES, UNPEELED

1 SPRIG OF THYME, LEAVES PICKED

2 TABLESPOONS COARSELY CHOPPED FLAT-LEAF PARSLEY

1 TABLESPOON COARSELY CHOPPED MINT

SEEDS FROM 1 POMEGRANATE

½ CUP SLICED PISTACHIOS

1 TABLESPOON POMEGRANATE MOLASSES

1 TO 2 TABLESPOONS PISTACHIO OR EXTRA VIRGIN OLIVE OIL

½ TEASPOON GROUND SUMAC

Equipment

FINE-MESH NYLON SIEVE

PIECE OF CLEAN CHEESECLOTH

Season the yogurt with salt and black pepper. Line a fine-mesh nylon sieve with the cheesecloth and scoop the seasoned yogurt into the lined sieve. Suspend the sieve over a bowl, cover with plastic wrap, and leave in the fridge for 24 hours to allow the water to drain from the yogurt.

Preheat the oven to 375°F. Scrub the carrots and beets and remove the stalks and leaves. Cut any large carrots in half and add to a roasting pan, drizzle with the oil, and season with salt and black pepper. Tuck the garlic cloves in with the carrots, scatter with the thyme, and roast on the middle rack of the oven for about 30 minutes, depending on size, until tender.

Cook the unpeeled beets in a saucepan of boiling salted water until tender, drain, and leave until cool enough to handle. Peel and cut into bite-sized wedges.

Put the carrots and beets into a bowl, add the chopped herbs, squeeze in the roasted garlic from its skin, and season with salt and black pepper. Mix the veggies gently using your hands and arrange on a serving platter. Dot the labneh over the top and scatter with the pomegranate seeds and pistachios. Drizzle over the pomegranate molasses and pistachio or olive oil and season with a sprinkling of the sumac. Serve immediately.

Chocolate and Pomegranate Pudding with Cocoa and Almond Nib Wafers

These chocolate puddings are simple yet elegant, the pomegranate giving an intriguing twist to a classic dinner party dessert. I like to serve something crisp alongside rich, creamy desserts and these cocoa nib wafers do the job nicely. The delicate cookies will soften in damp air or humidity, so make them on the day you plan to serve them and, once cooled, store in an airtight container between layers of parchment paper; the recipe makes around 20.

SERVES 6

2 LARGE POMEGRANATES

2 TEASPOONS GRANULATED SUGAR

7 OUNCES DARK CHOCOLATE, 70% COCOA SOLIDS, FINELY CHOPPED

1½ CUPS HEAVY CREAM

A PINCH OF SALT

½ TEASPOON VANILLA EXTRACT

1 MEDIUM EGG YOLK, LIGHTLY BEATEN

For the wafers

5 TABLESPOONS UNSALTED BUTTER

1 TABLESPOON HONEY

½ CUP GRANULATED SUGAR

⅓ CUP ALL-PURPOSE FLOUR

2 OUNCES COCOA NIBS

⅓ CUP ALMONDS

A PINCH OF SALT

Cut one of the pomegranates in half and press the fruit though an orange juicer to extract as much juice as possible from the seeds. Pour the juice into a small saucepan, add the sugar, and stir to dissolve. Bring the juice to a boil over medium heat and continue to cook for about 1 minute until reduced by half and thickened and syrupy.

Put the chocolate in a bowl. In a separate saucepan, bring the cream with the salt and vanilla to a boil and then simmer for 20 seconds before pouring in the chocolate. Add half the pomegranate syrup (reserve the remainder for serving) and, using a rubber spatula, stir gently until the chocolate has melted and the ganache is silky smooth. Add the egg yolk and mix until combined. Divide the mixture between six small glasses. Let cool and then cover with plastic wrap and chill in the fridge until set.

To make the wafers, melt the butter with the honey and sugar in a small saucepan over low to medium heat. Remove from the heat and let cool for 3 to 4 minutes before adding the remaining ingredients. Mix until thoroughly combined and then leave for at least 1 hour until firm. The dough can be made, covered, and chilled up to 24 hours before you plan on baking the wafers.

Preheat the oven to 350°F. Line two large baking sheets with parchment paper.

You will need to bake the wafers in small batches of 4 or 5 at a time. Spoon small cherry-sized balls of the dough onto each lined baking sheet and flatten into a neat disc using either your fingers or a palette knife. Bake on the middle rack of the oven for 6 to 7 minutes or until golden brown and bubbling. Remove from the oven and let cool and harden on the pans.

To serve, divide the reserved syrup between the glasses, top with the seeds from the remaining pomegranate, and serve with the wafers.

Turkish Pide with Lamb and Pomegranate Seeds

Pide is the Turkish equivalent of pizza, and these examples are topped with a delicious combination of aromatic spiced ground lamb, salty feta, smoky peppers, and a final contrasting flourish of fresh, juicy pomegranate seeds. They are ideal for lunch or supper, and can be put together in very little time, especially if you prepare the lamb topping in advance.

MAKES 8 PIDE

For the topping

1 TABLESPOON OLIVE OIL

1 ONION, FINELY CHOPPED

2 GARLIC CLOVES, CRUSHED

1 TEASPOON GROUND CUMIN

½ TEASPOON GROUND CORIANDER

½ TEASPOON CAYENNE PEPPER

A PINCH OF GROUND ALLSPICE

¼ TEASPOON GROUND CINNAMON

¼ TEASPOON DRIED OREGANO

14 OUNCES LEAN GROUND LAMB

7 OUNCES CANNED OR FRESH CHOPPED TOMATOES

1 TABLESPOON POMEGRANATE MOLASSES

A PINCH OF SUGAR

3½ OUNCES ROASTED RED PEPPERS FROM A JAR (DRAINED WEIGHT), SLICED INTO STRIPS

¾ CUP FETA, CRUMBLED

2 TEASPOONS KALONJI (NIGELLA) SEEDS

SEEDS FROM 1 POMEGRANATE

1 ROUNDED TABLESPOON CHOPPED FLAT-LEAF PARSLEY

½ TEASPOON GROUND SUMAC

SALT AND FRESHLY GROUND BLACK PEPPER

For the dough

1¼ CUPS BREAD FLOUR, PLUS EXTRA FOR DUSTING

¼ OUNCE FAST-ACTION/EASY-BLEND DRIED YEAST

A PINCH OF GRANULATED SUGAR

A GOOD PINCH OF SEA SALT

2 TABLESPOONS OLIVE OIL, PLUS EXTRA

First begin preparing the topping: Heat the olive oil in a large frying pan, add the onion, and cook over medium heat until tender but not colored. Add the garlic, spices, and oregano and cook for another minute. Add the lamb and cook for about 5 minutes over medium to high heat until browned. Add the chopped tomatoes, pomegranate molasses, and sugar and season with salt and black pepper. Cook for another 20 minutes until the meat is tender and most of the moisture from the tomatoes has been cooked off. Remove from the heat, spoon off any excess fat, and let cool while you prepare the dough.

Put the flour into the bowl of a free-standing mixer fitted with a dough hook. Add the yeast, sugar, and salt and mix well until combined. Make a well in the middle and add ¾ to 1 cup warm water and the olive oil. Mix on medium speed for about 8 minutes until the dough is silky smooth and elastic. Turn onto a work surface and shape into a ball. Place in a lightly oiled bowl, cover with plastic wrap, and leave in a warm place for about 1 hour or until doubled in size.

Preheat the oven to 400°F and line 2 large baking sheets with parchment paper.

Turn the dough onto a lightly floured work surface, knead lightly, and divide into 8 even-sized pieces. Roll each piece out into an oval shape roughly the same size as a pita bread and about 1⁄16-inch thick. Divide the lamb mixture between the dough shapes, spooning it into the middle of dough and leaving a border all around. Twist the ends of the dough together so that the dough forms a "boat" shape that encases the lamb. Scatter the roasted pepper strips over the lamb along with the feta. Drizzle the pide with olive oil, sprinkle with the kalonji (nigella) seeds, and bake on the middle rack of the oven for about 20 minutes until the dough is puffed and golden brown.

Generously scatter the hot pide with the pomegranate seeds and chopped parsley, season with the sumac, and serve immediately with pickled green chiles.

Beef Short Ribs Braised in Pomegranate

This is one of my new favorite dishes, making the most of pomegranate in a triple hit of juice, molasses, and fresh seeds. I'll admit that I have a tendency to be a lazy cook—I often choose dishes that require the minimum of effort yet give a huge return in terms of flavor and deliciousness. Beef short ribs are ideal for just such a choice, as they almost look after themselves in the oven while they gently cook to melting tenderness in a pool of spiced fruity juices. The dish can also be half or fully prepared in advance; the ribs should be marinated overnight for the best outcome. Serve simply with some steamed rice and crisp garlicky greens.

SERVES 4 GENEROUSLY

4½ POUNDS BEEF SHORT RIBS

2 TEASPOONS CUMIN SEEDS

2 TEASPOONS CORIANDER SEEDS

1 ROUNDED TEASPOON ANCHO OR CHIPOTLE
CHILE POWDER

½ TEASPOON DRIED OREGANO

2 RED ONIONS, SLICED

3 GARLIC CLOVES, BRUISED

1 CINNAMON STICK

2 TABLESPOONS OLIVE OIL

1 TABLESPOON TOMATO PASTE

2 CUPS UNSWEETENED POMEGRANATE JUICE

2 CUPS GOOD RICH BEEF STOCK

2 TABLESPOONS POMEGRANATE MOLASSES

1 TO 2 TEASPOONS LIGHT BROWN SUGAR

SALT AND FRESHLY GROUND BLACK PEPPER

SEEDS FROM 1 POMEGRANATE

2 TABLESPOONS CHOPPED
FLAT-LEAF PARSLEY

2 TABLESPOONS CHOPPED CILANTRO

1 RED CHILE, FINELY CHOPPED

Slice the beef into individual ribs and place in a large bowl.

Heat a small frying pan over medium heat, add the cumin and coriander seeds, and toast for a minute or so until smoking and fragrant. Grind the seeds using a mortar and pestle, then mix in the chile powder, oregano, and a good seasoning of salt and black pepper. Turn over the ribs and add the onions, garlic, and cinnamon stick. Mix well using your hands, making sure that the spices are really well rubbed into the meat. Cover with plastic wrap and let marinate in the fridge overnight.

Preheat the oven to 300°F. Remove the ribs from the bowl, scraping off the onions and garlic and reserving them. Heat 1 tablespoon of the olive oil in a large frying pan, add the ribs, and brown well on all sides. Remove from the pan and transfer to a flameproof casserole or Dutch oven. Add the remaining tablespoon of oil to the frying pan and cook the onions and garlic until soft but not colored, stirring frequently to cook evenly. Add the tomato paste, mix well, and cook for another minute. Pour the pomegranate juice and stock into the pan, bring to a boil, and stir well to incorporate any browned bits on the bottom of the pan. Pour over the ribs and bring back to a boil. Cover with the lid and cook on the middle rack of the oven for about 2 hours until the meat is tender and almost falling off the bone.

Using a slotted spoon, remove the ribs from the casserole, cover with foil, and keep warm. Let the sauce rest and cool for 15 minutes and then spoon off any excess fat on top. Place the casserole over medium heat, add the pomegranate molasses, and reduce the sauce by half until thickened and glossy. Taste and add sugar, salt, and black pepper as needed. Return the ribs to the casserole, scatter with the pomegranate seeds, herbs, and chile, and serve immediately.

Gulab Jamun with Pomegranate and Pistachio

When traveling through India a few years ago, I used to treat myself to a gulab jamun whenever I saw them—often from a street vendor and served in a little banana leaf bowl. These Indian donut milk balls are deep-fried to a golden brown color and then completely drenched in a fragrant cardamom and rose syrup. I serve them with fresh, sharp pomegranate seeds to contrast the sweetness, and pistachios for a pop of color and crunch.

SERVES 8 TO 10

For the syrup

1¾ CUPS GRANULATED SUGAR

6 GREEN CARDAMOM PODS

1 CINNAMON STICK

1 TO 2 TEASPOONS ROSEWATER

2 TEASPOONS FOOD-GRADE DRIED ROSE PETALS (OPTIONAL)

For the gulab jamun

1 QUART SUNFLOWER OIL, FOR DEEP-FRYING

1½ CUPS DRY MILK POWDER

⅓ CUP ALL-PURPOSE FLOUR

A PINCH OF BAKING SODA

⅓ CUP WHOLE MILK, PLUS EXTRA IF NEEDED

⅓ CUP PLAIN YOGURT

2 TABLESPOONS MELTED CLARIFIED BUTTER

To serve

⅓ CUP SLICED PISTACHIOS

SEEDS FROM 1 POMEGRANATE

Equipment

SUGAR THERMOMETER

Start by making the syrup: Add the sugar and 2 cups of cold water to a large saucepan. Bruise the cardamom pods using a mortar and pestle and add to the pan with the cinnamon stick. Bring slowly to a boil to dissolve the sugar, then simmer for 2 minutes. Remove from the heat and stir in the rosewater and dried rose petals—use the rosewater cautiously, as it can be overpowering and vary in strength.

Pour the sunflower oil into a large pan, wok, or deep-fat fryer, pop a thermometer into the pan, and heat the oil to 300°F.

While the oil is coming up to temperature, prepare the gulab jamun: In a large mixing bowl, mix together the milk powder, flour, and baking soda. Make a well in the center and add the milk, yogurt, and all but 1 teaspoon of the clarified butter. Using your hand, quickly mix everything until smooth, adding a little extra milk if the mixture appears dry—it should be quite sticky but the milk powder will start to absorb the liquid as you mix. Working quickly, lightly grease the palm of your hands with a little of the reserved clarified butter, pinch off a walnut-sized nugget of dough, and roll into a totally smooth ball in your hands. Place on a parchment paper-lined pan and repeat until all the dough has been used up—you should end up with 20 to 24 balls. Loosely cover the pan with a slightly damp clean kitchen towel.

Once the oil has reached 300°F, bring the syrup back to a boil and then remove from the heat. Carefully drop 4 to 5 balls at a time into the hot oil, maintaining the heat at a steady 300°F, and cook for about 5 minutes, turning so that they cook to an even deep, amber golden brown and have almost doubled in size. Using a slotted spoon, scoop the gulab from the oil, drain briefly on paper towels, and then drop them into the hot syrup. If the syrup cools down, gently heat it without boiling. Let soak overnight at room temperature.

The next day, scoop out the cardamom pods, cinnamon stick, and rose petals and serve the gulab jamun with a spoonful of the syrup, scattered with the sliced pistachios and pomegranate seeds.

Malted Chocolate Banana Cake

This cake makes the most of those overripe bananas that I always seem to have idling in the fruit bowl, their condition making them perfect for baking; underripe bananas will give little or no flavor whatever you do to them. The cake keeps well in an airtight container and actually benefits from being baked the day before you plan on serving and frosting.

SERVES 10

14 TABLESPOONS UNSALTED BUTTER,
SOFTENED, PLUS
1 TABLESPOON, MELTED, FOR GREASING

⅓ CUP COCOA POWDER, PLUS 1 TABLESPOON
FOR DUSTING

2¼ CUPS ALL-PURPOSE FLOUR

3 TABLESPOONS MALTED MILK POWDER
(OVALTINE)

2 TEASPOONS BAKING POWDER

½ TEASPOON BAKING SODA

A GOOD PINCH OF FINE SEA SALT

4 MEDIUM, RIPE BANANAS

3 TABLESPOONS SOUR CREAM, AT ROOM
TEMPERATURE

1 TEASPOON VANILLA EXTRACT

⅔ CUP LIGHT BROWN SUGAR

½ CUP GRANULATED SUGAR

4 LARGE EGGS, BEATEN

2 OUNCES DARK CHOCOLATE,
FINELY CHOPPED

For the frosting

½ CUP LIGHT BROWN SUGAR

½ CUP DARK BROWN SUGAR

5 TABLESPOONS UNSALTED BUTTER

½ CUP HEAVY CREAM

2 OUNCES DARK CHOCOLATE, CHOPPED

½ TEASPOON VANILLA EXTRACT

A LARGE PINCH OF SEA SALT

Equipment

10-CUP BUNDT PAN

Preheat the oven to 350°F. Use the melted butter to coat the inside of the pan, making sure that you grease all the creases and ridges thoroughly. Dust the inside of the pan with an even coating of the extra 1 tablespoon cocoa and pour out any excess.

Sift together the remaining cocoa, flour, malted milk powder, baking powder, baking soda, and salt. In a separate bowl, mash the bananas, then add the sour cream and vanilla extract and mix to combine.

Using a free-standing mixer, cream the butter and both sugars together until pale, light, and fluffy. Gradually add the beaten eggs, mixing well between each addition and scraping down the sides of the bowl with a rubber spatula from time to time. Pour in the dry ingredients and banana mixture and mix until thoroughly combined. Add the chocolate and fold in using the spatula.

Spoon the mixture into the prepared pan, spread level, and bake in the oven on the rack just below the middle for 30 to 40 minutes until well-risen and a wooden skewer inserted into the middle comes out clean. Let the cake rest in the pan for no more than 2 minutes and then carefully turn onto a wire rack until completely cold.

To make the frosting, gently heat both sugars, butter, and cream in a small saucepan to dissolve the sugar and melt the butter, then bring to a boil. Simmer for 30 seconds, remove from the heat, and add the chocolate, vanilla, and salt. Stir until the chocolate has melted and the sauce is silky smooth. Carefully spoon the sauce over the cold cake, allowing it to drizzle over the sides, and let set before serving.

Sticky Spiced Pork Belly and Watermelon

This recipe is inspired by a dish served at Fatty Crab, a Malayasian-inspired restaurant in New York, where Zakary Pelaccio's Watermelon Pickle and Crispy Pork is permanently on the menu. My version is much simplified, although no less yummy, the pork being marinated overnight before cooking rather than being marinated, braised, and then fried. I've also done away with the pickled watermelon rind while still keeping the salad fresh and light. Chilling the melon before serving creates a refreshing contrast to the salty, spiced pork.

SERVES 4

3 GARLIC CLOVES, SLICED

2-INCH PIECE OF FRESH GINGER, SLICED

1 ROUNDED TEASPOON CHINESE FIVE-SPICE

2 TABLESPOONS DARK SOY SAUCE

2 TABLESPOONS HONEY

2 TABLESPOONS CHINESE BLACK
RICE VINEGAR

3.3 POUNDS BONELESS PORK BELLY,
SKIN SCORED

SEA SALT

For the salad

½ MEDIUM-SIZED WATERMELON,
CHILLED, RIND REMOVED, AND CUT INTO
BITE-SIZED CUBES

4 SCALLIONS, SLICED

1 LARGE RED CHILE, SEEDED AND SLICED

1½-INCH PIECE OF FRESH GINGER, CUT INTO
FINE MATCHSTICKS

3 TABLESPOONS SESAME OIL

2 TABLESPOONS SOY SAUCE

JUICE OF 1 LIME, PLUS EXTRA TO SERVE

2 TO 3 TEASPOONS BLACK OR TOASTED WHITE
SESAME SEEDS

3 TABLESPOONS COARSELY CHOPPED
CILANTRO

Start by marinating the pork: Put the garlic and ginger on a baking sheet or in a shallow bowl that will fit the pork belly lying flat and snuggly. Add the five-spice, soy sauce, honey, and vinegar and mix to combine. Lay the pork on the pan or in the bowl, skin-side up, cover with plastic wrap, and let marinate overnight in the fridge.

The next day, line a roasting pan with a double thickness of foil and sit a roasting or wire rack on top. Remove the pork from the marinade, lay on top of the rack, skin-side up, and leave for an hour at room temperature to dry the skin.

Preheat the oven to 425°F. Sprinkle the pork skin lightly with sea salt and roast for 20 minutes on the middle rack of the oven. Reduce the temperature to 350°F and cook the pork for another hour until the skin has crisped and the meat is cooked through.

Meanwhile, for the salad, put the prepared watermelon, scallions, chile, and ginger into a bowl and use your hands to very gently mix. Combine the sesame oil, soy sauce, and lime juice in a cup, but don't pour over the salad until just before serving, otherwise the watermelon will become soggy.

Once the pork is cooked, let it rest for 10 minutes and then cut into small bite-sized pieces. Pour the dressing over the salad and divide between serving plates. Arrange the pork on top, scatter with the sesame seeds and cilantro, and serve immediately with extra lime on the side.

Grilled Shrimp with Watermelon and Feta

This is really an amped-up Greek salad. Hot, sweet, and spiced shrimp are a wonderful contrast to chilled, juicy watermelon and salty feta. For best effect, serve this dish outside on a hot summer's day, with the shrimp cooked on the grill if you should happen to have it lit already.

SERVES 3 TO 4

16 RAW WHOLE JUMBO SHRIMP

2 LEMONS

3 GARLIC CLOVES, SLICED

½ TO 1 TEASPOON CRUSHED RED PEPPER

½ TO 1 TEASPOON DRIED OREGANO

SALT AND FRESHLY GROUND BLACK PEPPER

1 SMALL WATERMELON

1 CUP FETA, CRUMBLED

4 SCALLIONS, SLICED

¼ CUP FRUITY EXTRA VIRGIN OLIVE OIL

A GOOD HANDFUL OF GREEK BASIL OR MINT LEAVES

Equipment

BARBECUE OR RIDGED GRILL PAN

Start by marinating the shrimp: Put the shrimp into a large glass or ceramic bowl and add the juice and finely grated zest of 1 lemon, garlic, crushed red pepper, oregano, and a good seasoning of salt and black pepper. Mix well, cover, and let marinate in the fridge for a couple of hours.

While the shrimp are marinating, cut the watermelon into chunks or slices and remove the skin. Arrange on a large platter, cover, and chill in the fridge.

Preheat a grill or ridged grill pan on the stove over medium to high heat. Cook the shrimp for 1 to 2 minutes on each side until cooked through and nicely charred. Arrange the shrimp over the chilled watermelon and scatter with the feta and scallions. Drizzle the olive oil over the whole dish, top with a flourish of Greek basil or mint, and serve with extra lemon to squeeze over.

Melon Sangria

You could add a dash of brandy or Cointreau to this refreshing summer punch if you want to pep it up somewhat.

½ CHARENTAIS OR CANTALOUPE MELON

½ HONEYDEW MELON

1 CRISP, SWEET APPLE

A GOOD HANDFUL OF SEEDLESS
GREEN GRAPES

750-MILLILITER BOTTLE DRY WHITE WINE

½ CUCUMBER

2 CUPS SPARKLING WHITE WINE, SODA WATER,
OR LEMONADE

ICE, TO SERVE

Peel, seed, and finely slice the melons, then transfer into a large pitcher. Quarter, core, and slice the apple, cut the grapes in half, and add to the melons. Pour in the white wine and mix to combine. Cover and chill in the fridge for a couple of hours.

Cut the cucumber into thin slices and add to the pitcher with the sparkling wine, soda water, or lemonade. Add plenty of ice and pour into tall glasses to serve.

Watermelon Margarita

I have to thank my boyfriend Hugh for this recipe and for undertaking the not-so-onerous task of coming up with what he thinks is the correct balance of juice to tequila. You may need to adjust and tweak the sugar and lime according to the sweetness of your watermelon.

SERVES 4

½ SMALL WATERMELON

4 TEASPOONS GRANULATED SUGAR, PLUS
EXTRA IF NEEDED, TO TASTE

5 OUNCES GOLD TEQUILA

JUICE OF 2 LIMES, PLUS EXTRA IF NEEDED, TO
TASTE AND TO SERVE

To serve

COARSELY GROUND SEA SALT,
FOR THE GLASSES

ICE CUBES OR CRUSHED ICE

SMALL LIME WEDGES

Cut the watermelon into wedges, remove the rind and any seeds, and blend the flesh with the sugar in a blender or using an immersion blender until smooth. Pour 2 cups juice into a pitcher, add the tequila and lime juice, and mix well. Taste and add more sugar and lime juice accordingly.

Sprinkle a layer of salt onto a side plate. Rub the rim of each glass with a little lime juice and dip into the salt to coat. Fill the glasses with ice cubes or crushed ice, pour in the watermelon mixture, and serve immediately with a small lime wedge on the side.

Melon and Papaya Salad with Lemongrass and Ginger Syrup

This vibrant, cooling, and colorful fruit salad makes the most of the variety of melons that are in season at the height of summer. I would suggest using a mixture of Charentais, honeydew, and Galia for a good range of flavors and colors, but you can use what is readily available to you.

SERVES 6

¼ CUP SUPERFINE SUGAR

1 LEMONGRASS STALK, TRIMMED

2 LIME LEAVES

JUICE OF 1 LIME

2-INCH PIECE OF FRESH GINGER, SLICED

3 MIXED MELONS

1 RIPE PAPAYA

½ FRESH COCONUT

A HANDFUL OF REGULAR OR PINEAPPLE MINT LEAVES, COARSELY CHOPPED

Start by making the syrup, as it will need to infuse and cool before adding to the melons: Put the sugar in a small saucepan and add ½ cup water. Bruise the lemongrass stalk by bashing it with the flat blade of a large knife so that it breaks and tears slightly but still holds together. Add to the pan with the lime leaves, lime juice, and ginger. Place over low heat to slowly dissolve the sugar, then bring to a boil. Simmer for 1 minute before removing from the heat and leaving until cold.

Cut the melons in half and scoop out the seeds using a spoon. Cut one half of each melon into wedges, cut away the rinds, and arrange on a serving plate. Cut the remaining melon into bite-sized pieces or shape into balls using a melon baller. Scatter the melon pieces or balls over the wedges. Cut the papaya in half, scoop out the seeds, and remove the skin, then cut the fruit into thin slices. Scatter over the melon.

Crack the coconut, drain the coconut water into a glass, and save as a cook's perk to enjoy later. Scoop out the coconut flesh and pare into thin strips using a vegetable peeler.

Strain the syrup over the melon and let infuse for 30 minutes, then scatter with the coconut and mint to serve.

To check a melon for ripeness, pick it up in your hands—it should feel heavy and the underside will smell deeply fragrant if it's ripe and ready to eat.

Fish Tacos with Persimmon Salsa

I first tasted fish tacos on the beach in the Hamptons after a long, strenuous day sunbathing and watching the surfers. They were served with a classic pico de gallo salsa of tomatoes, onions, and chile, but here I've added diced sweet persimmon and avocado. Have all of the elements prepared and ready to assemble before you start frying the fish and shrimp—tacos should be eaten immediately after making to fully enjoy the crispy fried fish.

SERVES 4 TO 6

For the persimmon salsa

1 LARGE RIPE PERSIMMON

2 TOMATOES, DICED

1 RIPE AVOCADO, DICED

1 RED CHILE, SEEDED AND FINELY DICED

3 SCALLIONS, SLICED

2 TABLESPOONS CHOPPED CILANTRO

JUICE OF 1 LIME, PLUS EXTRA LIMES TO SERVE

SALT AND FRESHLY GROUND BLACK PEPPER

For the cabbage coleslaw

1 GARLIC CLOVE, CRUSHED

8 TABLESPOONS MAYONNAISE

2 TABLESPOONS CHIPOTLE PASTE

½ SMALL WHITE CABBAGE, VERY FINELY SHREDDED

For the fish tacos

1 QUART SUNFLOWER OIL

18 OUNCES SOLE OR SNAPPER FILLETS

16 RAW LARGE PEELED SHRIMP

6 SOFT CORN TORTILLAS

For the batter

1 CUP ALL-PURPOSE FLOUR

2½ TABLESPOONS CORNSTARCH OR FINE POLENTA

1 TEASPOON BAKING POWDER

½ TEASPOON CAYENNE PEPPER

½ TEASPOON ANCHO OR MEDIUM CHILE POWDER

A GOOD PINCH OF GROUND ALLSPICE

½ TEASPOON DRIED OREGANO

1 TO 1¼ CUPS COLD BEER OR SPARKLING MINERAL WATER

Equipment

SUGAR THERMOMETER

RIDGED GRILL PAN (OPTIONAL)

Start by preparing the salsa: Using a vegetable peeler, remove the skin from the persimmon, then dice the flesh and add to a bowl. Add the tomatoes, avocado, chile, scallions, cilantro, and lime juice, season with salt and black pepper, and set aside.

Prepare the cabbage coleslaw: In a small bowl, mix the garlic with 6 tablespoons of the mayonnaise and the chipotle paste, season, and set aside. In a medium bowl, mix the cabbage with the remaining 2 tablespoons mayonnaise, season, and set aside.

Pour the sunflower oil into a large pan, wok, or deep-fat fryer, pop in a thermometer, and heat the oil to 350 to 375°F. Cover a baking sheet with a triple thickness of paper towels. Preheat the oven to 300°F.

When the oil has almost come up to temperature, prepare the batter: Sift the flour, cornstarch or polenta, baking powder, and spices into a large mixing bowl and add the oregano and a really good seasoning of salt and black pepper. Make a well in the middle of the dry ingredients and add the cold beer or sparkling water. Using a balloon whisk, very gently combine the batter—it should still be quite lumpy and most definitely not smooth, adding a little more liquid if it appears too thick. Dip the fish fillets and shrimp one at a time into the batter to completely coat, allowing any excess batter to drip back into the bowl, and cook in the hot oil in batches (to avoid overcrowding and cooling the oil) for 1 to 2 minutes until crisp and golden. Using a slotted spoon, remove from the oil and drain on the paper towel-covered pan. Keep warm in the oven while you cook the remaining batches.

Warm the tortillas either on a hot ridged grill pan over medium heat for about 30 seconds each side, or wrapped in foil in the oven for about 10 minutes. Pile the warm tortillas with a spoonful of the cabbage coleslaw, fish fillets, shrimp, and salsa and serve the chipotle mayo and limes alongside.

Persimmon and Ginger Spiced Cookies

Look out for really ripe, sweet persimmons for this recipe and use fruits that are roughly the size of an apple to yield the correct amount of purée.

MAKES ABOUT 30

2 LARGE RIPE PERSIMMONS

½ CUP SUNFLOWER OIL

⅓ CUP BLACKSTRAP MOLASSES

2½ CUPS ALL-PURPOSE FLOUR

⅔ CUP GRANULATED SUGAR

1 TEASPOON BAKING POWDER

1 TEASPOON BAKING SODA

1½ TEASPOONS GROUND GINGER

½ TEASPOON GROUND CINNAMON

A GOOD GRATING OF NUTMEG

A PINCH OF SALT

¾ CUP GRANULATED SUGAR, FOR ROLLING

Using a small sharp knife remove the skin from the persimmons and process the flesh in a mini blender until almost smooth. Scoop the pulp into a small pan and place over low heat. Stir constantly with a rubber spatula to prevent the purée from scorching on the bottom of the pan and cook until the purée has reduced by half to about 5 ounces.

Remove from the heat, transfer to a bowl, and add the sunflower oil and molasses and mix until smooth. Let cool for 2 to 3 minutes.

Sift the flour, granulated sugar, baking powder, baking soda, spices, and salt into large bowl and make a well in the center. Add the persimmoms mixture and beat until smooth.

Preheat the oven to 350°F and line two baking sheets with parchment paper.

Pour the granulated sugar onto a baking sheet. Using your hands, roll the cookie dough into walnut-sized balls and roll each one in the granulated sugar until coated. Arrange 12 cookies on each baking sheet and flatten each one slightly with your fingers. Bake on the middle rack of the oven for 10-12 minutes until crisp but still slightly soft in the middle. Repeat with the remaining cookie dough.

Let cool on the pans for 1 minute and then transfer to a wire rack until cold.

Orchard

As the summer months draw to a close and berries, soft fruit, and juicy peaches start to seem a distant memory, fruit lovers like myself can take heart in the promise of an early fall harvest of apples, pears, and quinces. If you are lucky enough to have an apple tree or two in your garden, then you will be all too aware of the wonderful sight of them in full blossom in the springtime, and with that—weather depending—comes the promise of a good haul of fruit later in the year.

Over the last few years there has been a renewed interest in heritage orchard fruits, and the days of surviving on only Granny Smiths, Golden Delicious, and Conference pears are long gone. Us cooks are now blessed with apples in a huge range of sizes, sweetness, and color, and with over 2,000 varieties available we are spoiled for choice. The diversity of pears grown worldwide is also vast nowadays, encompassing more than 500 varieties. Given the enormity of the subject, this chapter can only scratch the surface of what could easily have been a book in itself.

Apples provide us with surely the most loved fall dessert of all—the humble apple pie. In its purest form of apples baked in a pastry crust, it is utterly delicious and has graced more Sunday lunch tables than we can ever imagine. But the apple is worthy of so much more than a simple pie, from the French chausson and tarte Tatin through to bars, cakes, and even tangy caramels. If you have more than one apple tree, it's more than likely that in a good year you will have been forced to turn a bumper crop and mountains of windfalls into chutney or relish, and here you'll find a fiery, smoked chile update on the preserve theme that is perfect for cold cuts and cheese. I myself have an apple press on my wish list so that we can turn our own apples into juice and cider next autumn.

Until relatively recently, the nearest most people got to quince was in the form of membrillo—an amber-colored paste usually served with cheese and hailing (in slightly various forms and with different names) from the Middle East and all across southern Europe, including Spain, France, Portugal, and Italy. The beautiful, ancient quince, with its slightly knobbly pear shape and glowing yellow skin that is often covered in a downy jacket, is a well-traveled fruit. It grows in Britain and throughout the Mediterranean but also as far afield as Iran, China, and Argentina, and can trace its origins to Ancient Greece and Rome. Traditionally regarded as a symbol of love and fertility, some believe that it was actually a quince that was given to Adam by Eve in the Garden of Eden.

The quince in its raw form is not only beautiful, but left in a bowl will perfume a whole room with a sweet aroma. Somewhat unpalatable raw due to its highly acidic character, once cooked, the quince flesh turns almost deep red in color and can be used in both sweet and savory cooking. Try adding a few slices to a spiced tagine-style stew. Or grate the fruit into a preserving jar and top off with either vodka or brandy, then let steep for several months, shaking the jar at regular intervals, and open and enjoy come Christmas time.

Apple and Smoked Trout Salad with Hazelnuts and Celery

I like salads with a bit of snap and crunch, especially if they are being served as a main course, and I also like a splash of color and a zippy dressing. This salad meets all those criteria but needs to be made with sparkly fresh veggies—those that have been lurking in the back of the fridge simply will not do. Look out for fresh celery, along with apples and beets, as they are all in season at the same time. For best results, you'll need a mandolin slicer for the preparation of this salad, but if you don't have one, a sharp knife will suffice.

SERVES 4

A HANDFUL OF SHELLED HAZELNUTS

1 MEDIUM PINK OR CANDY-STRIPED BEETS

¼ CUCUMBER

2 CRISP, SHARP APPLES, SUCH AS GRANNY SMITH

6 RADISHES

2 CELERY STALKS

9 OUNCES SMOKED TROUT FILLETS

JUICE OF ½ LEMON

5 TABLESPOONS EXTRA VIRGIN OLIVE OIL

1 TEASPOON GRAINY DIJON MUSTARD

SALT AND FRESHLY GROUND BLACK PEPPER

3 TABLESPOONS SALAD CRESS

Coarsely chop the hazelnuts. Peel the beets and slice wafer thinly, using a mandolin if you can, followed by the cucumber. Quarter and core the apples, then slice in the same way. Slice the radishes into thin discs, and cut the celery into fine matchsticks.

Arrange the veggies and apples on serving plates and flake the smoked trout alongside or over the top.

In a small bowl, lightly whisk together the lemon juice, olive oil, and mustard, then season well with salt and black pepper. Drizzle the dressing over the salads, scatter with the salad cress, and serve.

Slow-roasted Pork with Spiced Apple Relish and Cider Gravy

A great roast pork dish with salty, super-crunchy crackling is not only a thing of beauty but a spectacularly good crowd pleaser, whether it be for Sunday lunch or served around a bonfire shredded into crusty bread rolls with a drizzle of the warm pan juices, a handful of arugula, and a good helping of the apple relish. More often than not you'll be fighting hands away from the meat as you're carving. Pay a visit to your local friendly butcher for a really good cut of meat that has been well prepared and comes from a pig that has been reared with care and attention. Apples feature three ways in this dish: apple relish that is cooked in the oven alongside the meat, in stuffing balls, and as a rich cider gravy.

SERVES 6 TO 8

For the pork

2 TEASPOONS FENNEL SEEDS

1 TEASPOON CORIANDER SEEDS

1 TEASPOON BLACK PEPPERCORNS

1 TEASPOON CRUSHED RED PEPPER

½ TEASPOON DRIED OREGANO

3 TEASPOONS SEA SALT, PLUS EXTRA

4 GARLIC CLOVES, CRUSHED

FINELY GRATED ZEST OF 1 LEMON

6½ POUNDS BONE-IN PORK LOIN, CHINED AND SKIN DEEPLY SCORED

1 TO 2 TABLESPOONS OLIVE OIL

FRESHLY GROUND BLACK PEPPER

For the stuffing

1 ONION, FINELY CHOPPED

1 FAT GARLIC CLOVE, CRUSHED

1 CRISP, SWEET APPLE, PEELED, CORED, AND COARSELY GRATED

10 SAGE LEAVES, FINELY CHOPPED

½ TEASPOON FENNEL SEEDS

14 OUNCES GOOD-QUALITY SAUSAGE MEAT

1 CUP FRESH WHITE BREAD CRUMBS

1½ OUNCES SLICED PANCETTA, FINELY CHOPPED

SALT AND FRESHLY GROUND BLACK PEPPER

For the relish and gravy

2 TART APPLES, PEELED, QUARTERED, AND CORED

3 TABLESPOONS UNSALTED BUTTER

1 ROUNDED TABLESPOON GRANULATED SUGAR

1 CINNAMON STICK

A PINCH OF CRUSHED RED PEPPER

A GRATING OF NUTMEG

2 CUPS HARD CIDER

1 TABLESPOON ALL-PURPOSE FLOUR

SALT AND FRESHLY GROUND BLACK PEPPER

Preheat the oven to 425°F.

Get the pork ready for the oven first: Using a mortar and pestle, lightly crush the fennel and coriander seeds and black peppercorns. Add the crushed pepper, oregano, salt, garlic, and lemon zest and mix to a paste. Push the mixture into the slits in the pork skin using your fingers. Place the pork, skin-side up, in a roasting pan and rub the skin with the olive oil. Season well with sea salt and black pepper and roast on the middle rack of the oven for 20 to 25 minutes until the skin starts to crisp.

Meanwhile, prepare the stuffing: Cook the onion in a tablespoon of olive oil in a frying pan until soft but not colored. Add the garlic, cook for another minute, then transfer to a bowl and let cool slightly. Add the remaining ingredients, season well and, using clean hands, combine thoroughly. Roll the mixture into 12 to 16 balls, arrange on a baking sheet, cover with plastic wrap, and chill for 30 minutes.

Turn the oven down to 350°F and cook the pork for another 2 hours.

Meanwhile, prepare the relish: Place the apple quarters in a small roasting pan, dot each with a pat of the butter, sprinkle with the sugar, add the cinnamon stick, crushed pepper, and nutmeg, and splash in 3 tablespoons of the

cider. Cover with foil and cook in the oven for about 25 minutes until the apples are tender and have reduced to a thick pulp. Remove from the oven, taste, and add a little more sugar if needed.

Turn the oven up to 425°F, add the stuffing balls to the oven and continue to cook the pork for another 20 to 25 minutes until the skin is very crisp and the stuffing balls are golden brown. Transfer the pork and stuffing to a serving dish, cover with foil, and let rest for

15 minutes. Spoon off all but 1 tablespoon of the fat from the pan and place over low heat. Stir in the flour, cook for 30 seconds, then add the remaining cider. Bring to a boil, stirring constantly and incorporating any bits from the bottom of the pan. Taste and season with salt and black pepper, and perhaps a little sugar to balance the acidity from the cider.

Slice the pork and serve with the apple relish, stuffing, and cider gravy. And don't forget the crackling.

Gingerbread Spiced Apple Donuts

These delicately spiced donuts are filled with tart apple purée and coated in either sugar or a lip-smacking lemon glaze. I make them slightly smaller than normal so that eating two (or three) in one sitting doesn't seem at all greedy.

MAKES ABOUT 16 SMALLISH DONUTS

For the filling

1 MACINTOSH APPLE, PEELED AND COARSELY CHOPPED

3 SMALL SWEET APPLES, PEELED AND COARSELY CHOPPED

JUICE OF ½ LEMON

2 TABLESPOONS GRANULATED SUGAR

3 TEASPOONS UNSALTED BUTTER

For the donuts

¾ CUP WHOLE MILK

¼ CUP LIGHT BROWN SUGAR

½ OUNCE ACTIVE DRIED YEAST (NOT FAST-ACTION/EASY-BLEND)

3½ CUPS BREAD FLOUR, PLUS EXTRA FOR DUSTING

1 TEASPOON GROUND CINNAMON

½ TEASPOON GROUND GINGER

A GENEROUS PINCH OF GROUND CLOVES

A GOOD GRATING OF NUTMEG

½ TEASPOON SEA SALT

1 LARGE EGG, BEATEN

1 LARGE EGG YOLK

1 ROUNDED TABLESPOON BLACKSTRAP MOLASSES

5 TABLESPOONS UNSALTED BUTTER, SOFTENED

1½ QUARTS SUNFLOWER OR PEANUT OIL

⅔ CUP GRANULATED SUGAR

JUICE OF ½ LEMON

3 TO 5 TABLESPOONS CONFECTIONERS' SUGAR

Equipment

2½-INCH PLAIN COOKIE CUTTER

SUGAR THERMOMETER

LARGE PIPING BAG FITTED WITH A ½-INCH PLAIN NOZZLE

Put all the filling ingredients into a large saucepan, half cover, and cook over low to medium heat, stirring frequently, for 5 to 6 minutes until the apples become a soft pulp. Uncover and continue to cook, stirring frequently, until thickened. Remove from the heat and leave until cold.

To make the donuts, heat the milk until warm to the touch, add 1 teaspoon of the brown sugar and the yeast and whisk to combine. Leave in a warm place for about 5 minutes until a thick foam has formed on top of the milk.

Put the flour, remaining brown sugar, spices, and salt into the bowl of a free-standing mixer fitted with the dough hook. Make a well in the center and add the yeasty milk, whole egg, egg yolk, molasses, and butter. Mix steadily for about 5 minutes until the dough is smooth and elastic—it will still be slightly sticky. Shape into a smooth ball and place in a large, lightly oiled mixing bowl. Cover with plastic wrap and let rise in a warm, draft-free place for at least 1 hour or until the dough has doubled in size.

Transfer to a work surface and knead gently for 30 seconds to knock out any air bubbles. Lightly dust the work surface with flour and roll the dough out to a thickness of ½ to ¾-inch. Using the cutter, stamp out discs and arrange on two lightly floured baking sheets, leaving plenty of space between each one. Cover loosely with oiled plastic wrap and let rise again for 30 to 45 minutes.

Pour the oil into a large saucepan so that it comes at least 4 inches up the sides and heat to 350 to 375°F. Cover a large baking sheet with a triple thickness of paper towels and pour the granulated sugar into a large bowl. In a small bowl, mix the lemon juice and confectioners' sugar until smooth.

Fry the donuts in batches—4 at most—for about 2 minutes on each side or until deep golden brown. Remove and drain thoroughly on the paper towels before either tossing in the granulated sugar or brushing with the lemon glaze. Make sure the oil returns to temperature before frying the next batch. Cool on a wire rack.

Make a small incision in the side of each donut. Fill the piping bag with the apple mixture and pipe through the incision into the middle of each donut.

Apple Chaussons

The success of this recipe requires you to make puff pastry, but please stop for a moment before you turn the page or add store-bought puff pastry to your shopping list. It's really not tricky and the results more than make up for the small amount of effort and skill involved—once you've tasted the difference that homemade flaky, buttery pastry makes, you'll be convinced. Use firm, crisp, sweet apples for the filling, as they will retain some texture during baking.

MAKES 14 TO 16

For the puff pastry

1¼ CUPS ALL-PURPOSE FLOUR, PLUS EXTRA FOR DUSTING

¾ CUP BREAD FLOUR

A PINCH OF SEA SALT

17 TABLESPOONS UNSALTED BUTTER, CHILLED

1 MEDIUM EGG YOLK, LIGHTLY BEATEN

½ CUP ICED WATER

1 TEASPOON LEMON JUICE

1 MEDIUM EGG, BEATEN, TO GLAZE

For the filling

4 SWEET APPLES, SUCH AS BRAEBURN OR GOLDEN DELICIOUS, PEELED AND THINLY SLICED

3 TEASPOONS UNSALTED BUTTER

2 TABLESPOONS GRANULATED SUGAR

1 TABLESPOON LEMON JUICE

Equipment

4½-INCH FLUTED COOKIE CUTTER

For the puff pastry, combine the flours and salt in a mixing bowl, add 3 tablespoons chilled diced butter, and rub in using your fingertips. Make a well in the center and add the egg yolk. Mix the iced water with the lemon juice and add ⅓ cup, mixing with a round-bladed knife to bring the dough together—you may need to add a drop more liquid but the dough shouldn't be too wet. Gather into a ball and flatten into a rectangle. Cover with plastic wrap and chill for 1 hour.

Lightly dust the work surface with flour. Roll the dough into a rectangle three times as long as it is wide (6 × 18 inches), with one of the shortest sides nearest to you. Place the remaining 14 tablespoons butter between two sheets of parchment paper and, using a rolling pin,

flatten it into a neat square slightly smaller than one-third of the pastry rectangle. Place the butter on the middle section of pastry, fold the bottom third up over it, brush off the excess flour, and fold the top third down so that the butter is encased. Brush off any excess flour and turn the square 90 degrees clockwise. Roll into a similar-sized rectangle as before, trying to keep it as neat as possible, then again fold the bottom third up over the middle third and the top third down, brushing off excess flour each time. Lightly press the pastry edges together, turn 90 degrees clockwise, wrap in plastic wrap, and chill for 1 hour.

Repeat this rolling, folding, and turning twice more so that you have rolled it 5 times in total. Leave in the fridge for 2 hours before using.

Meanwhile, put the apples in a saucepan with the butter and sugar. Cover and cook over low heat for about 5 minutes until soft and tender but not mushy, stirring to prevent the apples from sticking to the base of the pan. Add the lemon juice and let cool.

Roll out the pastry on a lightly floured work surface to a thickness of 1/16 inch and, using the cutter, stamp out discs. Spoon a tablespoonful of filling into a mound onto one half of each disc. Brush the other half with a little cold water, fold over the filling, and press the edges together to seal. Using a small knife, crimp up the edges, brush the pastry with the beaten egg, and arrange on parchment paper-covered baking sheets. Chill for 30 minutes.

Preheat the oven to 375°F. Brush the pastries again with eggwash and, using the tip of a small sharp knife, score a leaf pattern into the pastry, being careful not to cut all the way through. Bake on the middle shelf for 20 to 25 minutes until well-risen and golden brown. Serve warm or at room temperature.

Apple Tarte Tatin

I had not intended to include an apple pie as such in this book, my thinking being that the world did not need another recipe for such a classic. But when I got to thinking about my favorite apple pie—both to make and eat—tarte Tatin was top on the list. It's traditionally made with either puff pastry or a rich shortcrust, but I've come up with what I think is a far better option. This cream cheese dough is not only just about the easiest dough to make, it's utterly delicious. The quantities of butter and cream cheese might look excessive, but trust me—this is one helluva crust that is more than capable of standing up to the punch of the caramelized apples.

SERVES 6

For the cream cheese pastry dough

1⅓ CUPS ALL-PURPOSE FLOUR, PLUS EXTRA FOR DUSTING

A PINCH OF SEA SALT

14 TABLESPOONS UNSALTED BUTTER, CHILLED AND DICED

6 OUNCES FULL-FAT CREAM CHEESE

For the top

5 TABLESPOONS UNSALTED BUTTER, AT ROOM TEMPERATURE

⅓ CUP GRANULATED SUGAR

6 TO 8 FIRM SWEET APPLES, SUCH AS MACINTOSH, BRAEBURN, OR GOLDEN DELICIOUS, PEELED, CORED, AND QUARTERED

CRÈME FRAÎCHE, TO SERVE

Equipment

9-INCH CAST-IRON OR OVENPROOF FRYING PAN

12 TO 14-INCH PLATE OR PAN, AS A GUIDE FOR CUTTING

To make the dough, put the flour and salt in the bowl of a food processor, add the butter, and pulse for 5 seconds—just long enough to cover the butter pieces in flour. Add the cream cheese in teaspoonfuls and pulse again until the butter and cream cheese have nearly been rubbed into the flour—you still want to see flecks of both.

Transfer to a lightly floured work surface and lightly knead to bring the dough into a slightly raggedy ball. Flatten into a fat disc, cover with plastic wrap, and chill for at least 2 hours.

Preheat the oven to 375°F. Smear the butter evenly over the base and sides of the frying pan, sprinkle with the sugar, then arrange the apple quarters in tight concentric circles, core-side up, on top. Set the pan over medium heat and cook the apples without stirring or moving them for 8 to 10 minutes until the butter and sugar have melted and started to caramelize. Check by carefully lifting one apple quarter and peeking at the underside—it should be tinged with golden brown caramel. Remove from the heat.

Lightly dust the work surface with flour. Roll out the dough and, using the plate or pan guide, cut into a 12 to 14-inch disc, then trim the edges to neaten. Carefully lift and place the dough over the apples, then using a palette knife, carefully push the edges down into the pan around the inside rim so that they are encased in a dough pillow. Return the pan to medium heat for 1 minute so that the dough just starts to seal and cook around the edges, then slide onto the middle rack of the oven and bake for 25 to 30 minutes until the crust is golden brown, crisp, and flaky.

Let cool in the pan for 2 minutes, then run a palette knife around the edge to loosen. Place a serving plate on top of the pan and, holding the pan and plate firmly with an oven mitt, flip over so that the tart turns onto the plate. Serve immediately with crème fraîche.

Apple Caramels

If you are lucky enough to have an apple tree or two, you will be all too aware of the inevitable glut that a good harvest brings. Here's a way to use up a number of apples when you have tired of apple pies and juicing.

MAKES 30 TO 40

1 QUART CLOUDY UNPASTEURIZED OR FRESHLY SQUEEZED AND FILTERED APPLE JUICE

1 CINNAMON STICK

1 TO 2 STAR ANISE

2 CLOVES

5 TABLESPOONS UNSALTED BUTTER, DICED, PLUS EXTRA FOR GREASING

¾ CUP LIGHT BROWN SUGAR

⅔ CUP GRANULATED SUGAR

½ CUP CRÈME FRAÎCHE

A GOOD PINCH OF SEA SALT

Equipment

7-INCH SQUARE BAKING PAN OR EQUIVALENT-SIZED RECTANGULAR PAN

SUGAR THERMOMETER

Grease and line the baking pan with parchment paper.

To make the apple caramel syrup, pour the apple juice into a large saucepan, add the whole spices, and bring to a boil. Cook steadily over low to medium heat until the juice has reduced to 4½ ounces of honey-colored syrup. Pick the spices out of the syrup before weighing to get an accurate measure, and note that it is easier to do this by weight rather than measure it by volume in a measuring cup.

Pour the syrup into a clean 2-quart saucepan and add the butter, both sugars, and the crème fraîche. Set the pan over low heat and stir frequently to melt the butter and dissolve the sugar. Add the thermometer to the pan, bring to a boil, and cook at a steady, even pace, stirring from time to time, until the syrup reaches 260°F. Slide the pan off the heat, then remove the thermometer, add the sea salt, and stir to combine with a rubber spatula.

Pour the syrup into the prepared pan and leave until completely cold before cutting into squares with a lightly greased knife and wrapping in twists of waxed or parchment paper. To make cutting easier, pop the caramel into the fridge for 1 hour to firm up. The caramels will keep for up to 1 week in an airtight box in the fridge.

To make the juice for the syrup, you can press the apples through a juicer and then filter through coffee filter papers, or use a fresh cloudy unpasteurized apple juice like those available from fruit farms. The reduced apple syrup is not only delicious in these caramels, but if you stop cooking the juice when it reaches 6 to 7 ounces, it makes a wonderful syrup to pour over cakes and pancakes, or try the Apple Caramel Crumb Bars on page 212.

Apple Caramel Crumb Bars

Everyone needs a recipe for apple crumble in their repertoire. It's also useful to be able to rustle up fruity bars for portable snacks or weekend treats. These bars tick all of those boxes and more besides. The apple caramel syrup really gives them a boost, but if you're not inclined to make it, you could substitute maple syrup at a pinch.

MAKES 12 TO 16 BARS

For the filling

6 CRISP, SWEET APPLES

JUICE OF ½ LEMON

½ TEASPOON GROUND CINNAMON

½ CUP APPLE JUICE

A PINCH OF SEA SALT

2 TEASPOONS CORNSTARCH

1⅓ CUPS ALL-PURPOSE FLOUR

⅓ CUP WHOLE-GRAIN SPELT FLOUR

⅔ CUP GRANULATED SUGAR

½ TEASPOON BAKING POWDER

A PINCH OF SEA SALT

12 TABLESPOONS UNSALTED BUTTER, CHILLED AND DICED, PLUS EXTRA FOR GREASING

1¼ CUPS ROLLED OATS

1 MEDIUM EGG YOLK

2 TABLESPOONS HEAVY CREAM OR WHOLE MILK

⅔ CUP WALNUTS, COARSELY CHOPPED

3 TABLESPOONS APPLE CARAMEL SYRUP (SEE PAGE 211) OR MAPLE SYRUP

Equipment

8 × 12-INCH BAKING PAN, 1½-INCHES DEEP

Start by making the filling: Peel, core, and slice the apples directly into a large saucepan, then add the lemon juice, cinnamon, half the apple juice, and the salt. Half cover and cook over medium heat for about 5 minutes until the slices are just tender but not mushy. In a small bowl, whisk together the cornstarch with the remaining apple juice. Add to the pan, stir well, and cook for 45 seconds to 1 minute until the mixture has thickened and the cornstarch has been cooked out. Slide the pan off the heat and let the apples cool to room temperature while you prepare the base and topping.

Grease the baking pan and line the bottom and sides with a large sheet of parchment paper. Preheat the oven to 350°F.

Put both flours into the bowl of a food processor and add the sugar, baking powder, and salt. Pulse to combine and then add the butter and pulse again until it has been rubbed into the dry ingredients. Add the rolled oats and pulse until combined and the mixture starts to clump together. Transfer to a large mixing bowl. Mix the egg yolk with the cream or milk and add to the crumble mix. Stir together using a palette knife and then your fingers until combined. Spoon three-quarters of the crumble mix into the prepared pan and press into an even layer with your hands to form the base. Bake on the middle rack of the oven for about 15 minutes until pale golden brown.

Mix the walnuts into the remaining crumble. Spoon the apple filling onto the base in an even layer, drizzle with the syrup, and scatter with the walnut crumble. Bake on the middle rack of the oven for about 30 minutes or until the crumble is golden brown and the apples are bubbling. Let cool completely and then cut into bars to serve.

Smoky Apple and Pear Relish

This snappy, fruity relish is just the ticket to serve with a nutty hard cheese or cold cuts. When cooking preserves and pickles, I tend to make smaller batches, as I find it easier and more accurate to double the quantities if I have a glut of fruit rather than having to reduce quantities to make a small number of jars. This also means that I can fill my cupboards with a nice variety of preserves rather than having groaning shelves of a single type.

MAKES 4 JARS

2 LARGE DRIED SMOKED CHIPOTLE CHILES

4 CRISP, SWEET APPLES, PEELED AND DICED

4 FIRM PEARS, PEELED AND DICED

1¾ CUPS CIDER VINEGAR

1⅔ CUPS LIGHT BROWN SUGAR

3 LARGE SHALLOTS, FINELY CHOPPED

2 GARLIC CLOVES, CRUSHED

1½-INCH PIECE OF FRESH GINGER, GRATED

1 TEASPOON FENNEL SEEDS

1 TEASPOON CAYENNE PEPPER

½ TEASPOON FRESHLY GROUND BLACK PEPPER

1 TEASPOON SEA SALT

Equipment

4 × 16-OUNCE CANNING JARS

Soak the chipotle chiles in a bowl of just-boiled water while you prepare the remaining ingredients.

Put the fruit in a large stainless steel saucepan and add all the other ingredients. Drain the chipotle chiles, remove the stems, and finely chop the chiles, seeds and all. Add to the pan and stir to combine. Set over low to medium heat and slowly bring to a boil, stirring from time to time. Continue to cook over low to medium heat for about 40 minutes or until the fruit is very tender and the liquid is reduced, thickened, and syrupy.

Slide the pan off the heat and spoon the chutney into the warm sterilized jars (see page 132), leaving ¼ to ½ inch headspace. Seal with the lids, process in a water bath (see page 40), and leave until cold before labeling. Store in a cool, dark cupboard for 1 month before opening, then store in the fridge and use within 2 months. The unopened chutney will keep for up to 6 months.

Homemade Yogurt with Honey-baked Apples and Pears and Granola

Clearly, it's not strictly necessary to make your own yogurt, but if you're anything like me then you'll get enormous satisfaction from sitting down to eat breakfast knowing that you've cooked all the elements from scratch. The yogurt and granola in this recipe will most likely make more than you need in one sitting but both will provide you with delicious homemade breakfasts for a week.

SERVES 6

For the yogurt

4 CUPS WHOLE ORGANIC MILK

⅓ CUP ORGANIC PLAIN LIVE YOGURT

For the granola

1¼ CUPS ROLLED OATS

½ CUP OR SPELT FLAKES

⅓ CUP WHOLE OR SLICED ALMONDS

⅓ CUP SHELLED UNSALTED PISTACHIOS

¾ TO 1 CUP MIXED SEEDS, SUCH AS PUMPKIN, SESAME, AND FLAXSEED

⅓ CUP HONEY

2 TABLESPOONS OLIVE OIL

1 TEASPOON VANILLA EXTRACT OR BEAN PASTE

¼ TEASPOON GROUND CINNAMON

A PINCH OF SEA SALT

For the compote

3 APPLES, QUARTERED AND CORED

2 PEARS, QUARTERED AND CORED

3 TABLESPOONS HONEY

1 TEASPOON VANILLA BEAN PASTE

3 TABLESPOONS UNSALTED BUTTER

A GOOD PINCH OF GROUND CINNAMON

A GOOD GRATING OF NUTMEG

Equipment

SUGAR THERMOMETER

LARGE MASON OR OTHER PRESERVING JAR

Start by making the yogurt: Pour the milk into a large saucepan, place over low to medium heat, and bring to 180°F. Immediately slide the pan off the heat, leaving in the thermometer, and let cool until the milk reaches 115°F. Add the yogurt and mix to combine, then pour into the warm sterilized preserving jar (see page 132). Seal with the lid, wrap the jar in a double or triple thickness of clean kitchen towels, and leave in a warm place such as at the side of the stove or on top of the oven for at least 4 hours and up to 12 until thickened—don't stir.

To make the granola, preheat the oven to 300°F and line a large baking sheet with parchment paper. Pour the oats, rye or spelt flakes, nuts, and seeds into a large mixing bowl. Add the remaining granola ingredients and mix well to combine. Spoon onto the baking sheet and toast in the oven for about 30 minutes until golden brown and crisp, stirring frequently to ensure that it cooks evenly. Let cool before scooping into a jar or airtight container.

For the compote, preheat the oven to 350°F and line a medium-sized baking pan with parchment paper. Add in the fruit, drizzle with the honey and vanilla bean paste, dot over the butter, and sprinkle with the spices. Mix gently to coat, then cook on the middle rack for about 40 minutes until the fruit is tender and burnished with golden, buttery caramel juices. Let cool slightly and then serve with the yogurt and granola for a mighty fine breakfast.

Rather like making sourdough bread where you add a starter to the dough, yogurt follows the same principle and you add live yogurt to warm milk to create a bacteria culture. It's easy to keep an ongoing supply—simply hold back 3 ounces from your first batch of yogurt to make the next.

If you don't want to use your oven to ferment the yogurt, pour it into a vacuum flask, seal, and leave until cooled and thickened. Transfer into clean jars and store in the fridge until needed.

Hibiscus Poached Pears

I first cooked and tasted this dish while working with Suzanne Zeidy, an inspirational Egyptian food writer and restaurateur, and this is my variation on her recipe. Dried hibiscus flowers are available in Middle Eastern food shops or from online suppliers and impart a wonderful, deep color and slightly floral note to the pears.

SERVES 6

6 RIPE BARTLETT OR CONFERENCE PEARS

1 OUNCE DRIED HIBISCUS FLOWERS

2 STRIPS OF LEMON RIND

2 STRIPS OF ORANGE RIND

1 CUP SUPERFINE SUGAR

1¼ CUPS SWEET ROSÉ WINE

2 STAR ANISE

Peel the pears using a vegetable peeler, leaving the stems intact.

Put the hibiscus flowers, strips of lemon and orange rind, sugar, and rosé wine into a large saucepan that will snuggly hold the pears in a single layer. Add the star anise and bring to a boil to dissolve the sugar. Carefully submerge the pears in the liquid, adding just enough water to cover them, then cover the surface of the liquid with a disc of parchment paper.

Cook the pears at a very gentle simmer for about 30 minutes or until they are tender. The cooking time will depend on the ripeness and size of the pears, so to check for doneness, push a small, sharp knife into a pear. Once they are cooked, remove from the heat but leave in the liquid until completely cold or until ready to serve. The longer you leave the pears in the liquid, the deeper the red coloring from the hibiscus flowers will penetrate the fruit.

Arrange the pears in a serving dish and strain some of the poaching liquid around them to serve.

Dried hibiscus flowers are more often used to make a delicious and refreshing herbal tea. The flowers are steeped in boiling water, which is then sweetened, strained, and the tea served cold over ice.

Chocolate Sablé Choux Buns with Pears and Chocolate Sauce

Chocolate and pears are a classic pairing, as are choux buns with chocolate sauce, so it makes sense to combine them all in one sweet morsel. The contrast with the caramelized pears and cream filling and the hot chocolate sauce is sublime.

MAKES 30 TO 35 SMALL BUNS; SERVES 6

For the sablé

3 TABLESPOONS UNSALTED BUTTER, SOFTENED

¼ CUP LIGHT BROWN SUGAR

⅓ CUP ALL-PURPOSE FLOUR

2 TABLESPOONS COCOA POWDER

A PINCH OF GROUND CINNAMON

A PINCH OF SEA SALT

For the choux buns

½ CUP MILK

5 TABLESPOONS UNSALTED BUTTER, DICED

A PINCH OF SEA SALT

1 TEASPOON GRANULATED SUGAR

1 CUP ALL-PURPOSE FLOUR

4 MEDIUM EGGS, LIGHTLY BEATEN

For the pears and sauce

4 PEARS, PEELED AND CUT INTO SMALL DICE

⅓ CUP GRANULATED SUGAR

2½ CUPS HEAVY CREAM

5 OUNCES DARK CHOCOLATE, CHOPPED

1 ROUNDED TABLESPOON LIGHT BROWN SUGAR

2 TABLESPOONS MARSALA

Equipment

LARGE PIPING BAG FITTED WITH A ¼-INCH PLAIN NOZZLE

½-INCH PLAIN COOKIE CUTTER

Start by preparing the sablé: Cream together the butter and sugar. Add the flour, cocoa, cinnamon, and salt and mix, then very lightly knead the dough in your hands until smooth. Flatten into a disc, place between two sheets of parchment paper, and roll out to a thickness of ¹⁄₁₆-inch. Chill for 1 hour.

For the choux buns, preheat the oven to 350°F and line two baking sheets with parchment paper. Place the milk, butter, salt, sugar, and ½ cup cold water in a saucepan over medium heat and stir to melt the butter. Bring to a boil, then immediately slide the pan off the heat and quickly sift in the flour. Using a wooden spoon, beat vigorously until the batter is smooth. Return to low heat and cook, stirring constantly, for another minute until the mixture is silky smooth and leaves the sides of the pan cleanly.

Pour into the bowl of a free-standing mixer and gradually add the eggs, mixing well until the batter is silky smooth and reluctantly drops off a spoon—you might not need all the egg. Scoop into the piping bag and pipe 30 to 35 small buns over the lined baking sheets, leaving space between each to allow for expansion. Using the cutter, stamp out the same number of discs from the sablé dough. Place one disc on top of each bun and bake on the middle rack for about 12 minutes until the buns are golden brown and puffed up and the sablé is crumbly. Make a hole in the side of each bun with a skewer and return to the oven for another minute to dry out the insides. Let cool on a wire rack.

Put the pears in a large frying pan, sprinkle with the granulated sugar, and place over medium heat. Cook, stirring frequently, for 3 to 4 minutes until the pears are tender and caramelized. Let cool.

Whip half the cream until it holds firm peaks. Put the remaining cream, chocolate, and brown sugar into a saucepan and heat over low heat, stirring constantly to melt the chocolate. Add the Marsala and stir until smooth. To serve, cut each choux bun in half, spoon the pears onto the bottom half, and top with whipped cream and the choux lid. Serve with the warm chocolate sauce.

Crème Caramels with Marsala Baked Pears

The addition of crème fraîche makes for a richer crème caramel. Like the pears, it can be made ahead of time, but the pears should be at room temperature when served. For a less labor-intensive dessert, you could serve the pears warm with vanilla ice cream and warm chocolate sauce.

SERVES 6

For the crème caramel

1¼ CUPS SUPERFINE SUGAR

1½ CUPS WHOLE MILK

1 VANILLA BEAN, SPLIT IN HALF LENGTHWISE

4 MEDIUM EGGS

2 MEDIUM EGG YOLKS

¾ CUP CRÈME FRAÎCHE

For the pears

6 SMALL RIPE PEARS, HALVED AND CORED USING A MELON BALLER

⅔ CUP GRANULATED SUGAR

1 VANILLA BEAN, SPLIT IN HALF LENGTHWISE, THEN CUT IN HALF AGAIN ACROSS THE MIDDLE

1 CINNAMON STICK

⅓ CUP BLANCHED HAZELNUTS

1 CUP MARSALA

JUICE OF 1 LEMON

Equipment

6 × 5-OUNCE RAMEKINS

FINE-MESH NYLON SIEVE

To make the crème caramel, heat ¾ cup of the sugar with 2 tablespoons of hot water in a small, heavy-bottomed saucepan over low heat and dissolve without stirring. Increase the heat slightly and continue to cook, brushing down the sides of the pan with a wet pastry brush if sugar crystals start to form. As the caramel starts to color, gently swirl the pan to ensure that it cooks evenly. When a deep amber color, and working quickly to prevent it from overcooking, divide it between the ramekins and leave until cold and hardened.

Pour the milk into the caramel pan, add the vanilla seeds and the pod, and bring slowly to a boil. The moment the milk starts to boil, remove from the heat and leave to infuse for 20 minutes.

In a large bowl, whisk together the whole eggs, yolks, and remaining sugar, but don't over-mix to avoid creating air bubbles. Mix in the crème fraîche. Reheat the milk over low heat and pour into the egg mixture, whisking to combine. Strain through a fine-mesh nylon sieve into a pitcher and set aside for 2 hours to allow the custard to settle and any air bubbles to disperse.

Preheat the oven to 300°F. Arrange the ramekins in a roasting pan and divide the custard equally between them. Slide the pan onto the middle rack and pour boiling water into the pan so that it comes halfway up the sides of the ramekins. Cook for 20 to 25 minutes until set with a very slight wobble in the middle. Carefully remove the crème caramels from the oven, leaving them in the bain-marie until completely cool, then cover with plastic wrap and chill overnight.

Preheat the oven to 350°F. Arrange the pears, cut-side up, in a roasting pan and sprinkle with the sugar. Pop the vanilla bean pieces in with the pears with the cinnamon stick and hazelnuts. Pour the Marsala, ½ cup cold water, and the lemon juice around the pears and bake on the middle rack of the oven for about 25 minutes until tender. Remove from the oven and let cool to room temperature.

To serve, run a palette knife around the edges of each ramekin to release the crème caramels and turn onto serving plates. Arrange the baked pears alongside and serve with the caramel and pear pan juices.

Spiced Ginger and Chocolate Cake with Salted Caramel Pears

Like most gingerbread cakes, this benefits from being baked 24 hours in advance of serving to allow the spices to mature. Setting a timer helps ensure it's cooked enough to hold the weight of the pears halfway through baking.

SERVES 8

10 TABLESPOONS UNSALTED BUTTER, PLUS EXTRA FOR GREASING

⅓ CUP CORN SYRUP

¼ CUP BLACKSTRAP MOLASSES

¾ CUP DARK BROWN SUGAR

2 OUNCES DARK CHOCOLATE, 70% COCOA SOLIDS, CHOPPED

⅔ CUP STOUT OR BOILING WATER

2 NUGGETS OF CANDIED GINGER, CHOPPED

½ TEASPOON BAKING SODA

1⅔ CUPS ALL-PURPOSE FLOUR

1 TEASPOON BAKING POWDER

3 TO 4 TEASPOONS GROUND GINGER

1 ROUNDED TEASPOON GROUND CINNAMON

½ TEASPOON GROUND PUMPKIN PIE SPICE

¼ TEASPOON FRESHLY GROUND BLACK PEPPER

A PINCH OF CHILE POWDER

A PINCH OF FINE SEA SALT

3 LARGE EGGS, BEATEN

For the pears

4 SMALL RIPE PEARS

1 TABLESPOON UNSALTED BUTTER

1 TABLESPOON GINGER SYRUP

For the sauce

½ CUP GRANULATED SUGAR

1¼ CUPS HEAVY CREAM

3 TABLESPOONS BOURBON

1 OUNCE DARK CHOCOLATE

A PINCH OF SEA SALT

Equipment

2-POUND LOAF PAN, 4 × 10 INCHES ACROSS THE TOP

Preheat the oven to 350°F and position a rack in the bottom third of the oven. Grease the loaf pan and line the bottom and sides with a strip of greased parchment paper.

In a large saucepan, heat the butter, corn syrup, molasses, sugar, chocolate, and stout over low heat, stirring frequently to dissolve the sugar and melt the butter. When smooth, remove from the heat, add the candied ginger and baking soda, then let cool.

Sift the flour, baking powder, spices, and salt into a large mixing bowl. Whisk the eggs into the syrup mixture and add to the dry ingredients in three batches, beating really well after each addition and again for 1 minute once all the syrup mixture has been incorporated. Pour the batter into the prepared pan and bake for 30 minutes (set a timer) while you prepare the pears.

Peel, quarter, and core the pears, leaving the stems intact, and put in a small roasting pan. Add the butter and ginger syrup (or 2 tablespoons granulated sugar), toss to coat, and cook the pears on the shelf above the cake for 15 to 20 minutes until tender and starting to caramelize at the edges.

After 30 minutes, remove the cake from the oven and arrange the pears on top—the cake should have cooked enough for them not to sink into and deflate it. Bake for another 30 minutes until well-risen and a skewer inserted into the middle comes out clean. Let cool in the pan for 30 minutes, then transfer to a wire rack until cold.

Once the cake is cold, prepare the sauce. Place the sugar in a heavy-bottomed saucepan, add 2 tablespoons cold water, and set over low heat to dissolve the sugar without stirring. Increase the heat and continue to cook the syrup until it becomes an amber-colored caramel. Slide the pan off the heat and slowly stir in the cream. Return to low heat to re-melt any hardened caramel. Add the bourbon, chocolate, and salt and heat until smooth and combined. Serve the cake with caramel sauce poured over.

Butternut Squash Soup with Pears and Chestnuts

There's something comforting about a large pot of soup simmering away on the stove. I love the sweet creaminess of butternut squash and the bright, orangey-yellow color of this soup is enough to lift the spirits on a dank autumn afternoon. Squash or pumpkin pairs beautifully with spiced salami or chorizo, or salty smoked bacon, but add some cooked chestnuts and sweet tender pears and the combination really sings.

SERVES 6 TO 8

1 LARGE ONION, DICED

1 SMALL LEEK, DICED

1 CELERY STALK, DICED

1 CARROT, PEELED AND DICED

2 GARLIC CLOVES, CHOPPED

5 SLICES OF PANCETTA, DICED

2 LARGE SPRIGS OF THYME

2 TABLESPOONS OLIVE OIL

2 TABLESPOONS UNSALTED BUTTER

1 MEDIUM BUTTERNUT SQUASH

3 RIPE Bartlett OR Conference PEARS

1 CUP COOKED, PEELED CHESTNUTS

3½ CUPS HOT CHICKEN STOCK, PLUS EXTRA IF NEEDED

SALT AND FRESHLY GROUND BLACK PEPPER

½ CUP HEAVY CREAM

5½ OUNCES Hungarian Mangalica SPICED SALAMI OR CHORIZO, DICED

Put the onion, leek, celery, carrot, garlic, and pancetta into a large pan. Add one of the thyme sprigs, 1 tablespoon of the olive oil, and the butter. Cook over low to medium heat for about 10 minutes until the veggies are tender but not colored.

While they are cooking, peel, seed, and dice the squash and peel, quarter, core, and dice two of the pears.

Add the squash to the pan with the pears and 3½ ounces of the chestnuts and cook for another 2 to 3 minutes. Pour in the stock and season well with salt and black pepper, then cover and bring to a boil. Reduce to a gentle simmer and cook for about 30 minutes until the squash is tender when tested with the tip of a knife.

Fish out the thyme sprig and blend the soup using an immersion blender until smooth. Add the cream and a little more stock if the soup is on the thick side, then taste for seasoning, adding more salt and pepper as required.

Peel, core, and dice the remaining pear and chestnuts. Heat the remaining 1 tablespoon of olive oil in a frying pan, add the salami or chorizo, and cook until starting to brown. Throw in the pear, chestnuts, and leaves from the remaining thyme sprig and cook for another minute or so until the pear is tender and caramelized.

Ladle the soup into bowls, top with a good spoonful of the pear and salami/chorizo mixture, and serve immediately.

Orchard Fruit Galette

Galettes are the easiest fruit tarts to prepare, requiring no special pans or skills. This dough uses a combination of plain and rye flours, which adds a nutty crispness, but you could also use spelt flour in place of rye if you prefer.

SERVES 6 TO 8

For the dough

1⅔ CUPS ALL-PURPOSE FLOUR, PLUS EXTRA FOR DUSTING

¾ CUP RYE FLOUR

A GOOD PINCH OF SEA SALT

14 TABLESPOONS UNSALTED BUTTER, CHILLED

½ CUP HAZELNUTS, FINELY GROUND

¼ CUP GRANULATED SUGAR

3 TABLESPOONS ICED WATER

2 TEASPOONS CIDER VINEGAR OR LEMON JUICE, PLUS EXTRA IF NEEDED

For the filling

JUICE OF 1 LEMON

½ CUP GRANULATED SUGAR, PLUS 3 TABLESPOONS

3 SMALL QUINCES

3 CRISP APPLES, PEELED, QUARTERED, AND THINLY SLICED

3 RIPE PEARS, PEELED, QUARTERED, AND THINLY SLICED

½ TEASPOON GROUND CINNAMON

3 TABLESPOONS UNSALTED BUTTER

1 TABLESPOON MILK

To make the dough, add the flours and salt to a large mixing bowl. Coarsely grate in the butter and, using a round-bladed knife, cut it into the flour, just so that it starts to be rubbed in. Then use your fingertips to lightly rub the butter into the flour, lifting the mixture up out of the bowl and letting it almost roll over your fingertips. You don't want to fully incorporate the butter—it should still be visible in the flour. Add the ground hazelnuts and sugar and lightly mix. Combine the iced water and vinegar or lemon juice in a cup and add almost all to the bowl. Mix, using the knife again, until the mixture starts to come together, adding more liquid if necessary. Gather the dough together, trying not to knead it, shape into a ball, and flatten into a disc, then cover with plastic wrap and chill for 2 hours.

Meanwhile, prepare the filling: Add 2 cups of cold water, the lemon juice, and ½ cup of sugar to a medium saucepan. Peel, quarter, and core the quinces one at a time and immediately drop into the pan. Place over medium heat and bring slowly to a boil to dissolve the sugar. Cover with a disc of parchment paper and simmer gently for about 25 minutes until tender. Let cool in the syrup.

Preheat the oven to 350°F. Line a baking sheet with parchment paper. Put the apple and pear slices in a large bowl. Drain the quince from the cooking syrup, cut each quarter into slices, and add to the bowl. Add 2 tablespoons of the sugar and the cinnamon and mix well.

Lightly dust the work surface with flour, roll out the dough into a disc 1⁄16-inch thick, and place on the lined baking sheet. Pile the fruit into the middle, leaving a border of 3 inches all around, and dot with the butter. Fold the dough up and around the fruit—don't worry too much about finesse for this tart. Brush the dough with the milk and scatter with the remaining sugar. Bake on the middle rack of the oven for 10 minutes, then reduce the temperature to 350°F and cook for another 25 to 30 minutes until the crust is golden and crisp and the fruit tender. Serve warm.

Quince and Almond Tart

In this recipe, poached and baked quinces are served alongside and in the middle of a rich almondy cake.

SERVES 8

JUICE OF 1 LEMON

¾ CUP SUPERFINE SUGAR

4 SMALL QUINCES

3 TABLESPOONS UNSALTED BUTTER

⅓ CUP HONEY

2 TABLESPOONS MARSALA

1 SMALL CINNAMON STICK

2 BAY LEAVES

2 STRIPS OF ORANGE PEEL

2 STRIPS OF LEMON PEEL

JUICE OF ½ ORANGE

For the shortbread base

1 CUP ALL-PURPOSE FLOUR

7 TABLESPOONS UNSALTED BUTTER, CHILLED
AND DICED

¼ CUP CONFECTIONERS' SUGAR, PLUS EXTRA
FOR DUSTING

A PINCH OF SALT

For the cake mixture

4 LARGE EGGS, SEPARATED

¾ CUP GRANULATED SUGAR

FINELY GRATED ZEST OF 1 LEMON

½ TEASPOON GROUND CINNAMON

1 TEASPOON ORANGE FLOWER WATER

2⅓ CUPS GROUND ALMONDS

A PINCH OF SALT

Equipment

8-INCH SPRINGFORM CAKE PAN

Pour 2½ cups of cold water into a medium saucepan and add the lemon juice and sugar. Peel and quarter the quinces one at a time and immediately drop into the pan—don't worry about removing the cores at this stage. Place over medium heat and bring slowly to a boil to dissolve the sugar. Cover the fruit with a disc of parchment paper and simmer gently for about 25 minutes until tender.

Prepare the shortbread base: Preheat the oven to 350°F and line the bottom of the pan with parchment paper. Put the flour, butter, confectioners' sugar, and salt into a food processor and pulse until the butter has been rubbed into the flour and the mixture starts to clump together. Transfer the crumbly dough into the prepared pan and, using your hands, press into an even layer covering the bottom. Bake on the middle rack of the oven for 12 to 15 minutes until pale golden.

Line a baking pan with parchment paper. Remove the quince quarters from the pan and arrange eight in the prepared pan, core-side up. Dot with the butter, spoon over the honey and Marsala, and tuck in the cinnamon stick, bay leaves, and orange and lemon peels. Add the orange juice and 2 tablespoons of the quince poaching liquid. Cover loosely with another sheet of parchment and bake on the middle rack of the oven for 40 minutes or until very soft when tested with the tip of a sharp knife. Let cool in the pan.

Core and slice the remaining poached quinces and scatter over the shortbread base. To make the cake mixture, whisk the egg yolks and sugar until thick, pale, and doubled in volume. Whisk in the lemon zest, cinnamon, and orange flower water. Fold in the ground almonds. In another bowl, whisk the egg whites with the salt until they hold stiff peaks, then carefully fold into the almond mixture until there are no streaks of egg white remaining. Spoon the mixture on top of the quince, spread level, and bake on the middle rack for 40 minutes until golden brown, well-risen, and a skewer inserted into the middle comes out clean. Let cool in the pan. Serve the cake in slices, dusted with confectioners' sugar, with the baked quinces.

Ham Hock and Pickled Quince Salad

Pickled quince will keep for weeks in the fridge and are a delicious accompaniment for cold cuts, the vinegary but aromatic fruit being especially good with ham. Try also adding them chopped to a stuffing for pork or lamb.

SERVES 6

For the pickled quinces

2⅓ cups cider vinegar

2 cups granulated sugar

4 cloves

3 juniper berries

4 black peppercorns

1 star anise

1 cinnamon stick

1 bay leaf

2 strips of rind from a lemon

4 quinces

For the ham hock

1 ham hock

1 onion, quartered

1 carrot, coarsely chopped

1 celery stalk, coarsely chopped

1 bay leaf

1 sprig of thyme

3 to 4 black peppercorns

1 tablespoon Dijon mustard

2 tablespoons honey

To serve

¾ cup walnuts

a bunch of watercress

1 small head of radicchio, leaves separated

5 tablespoons walnut oil

2 tablespoons cider vinegar

1 rounded teaspoon Dijon mustard

2 tablespoons coarsely chopped flat-leaf parsley

salt and freshly ground black pepper

Equipment

2 × 16-ounce canning jars

Start by preparing the pickled quinces: Add all the ingredients, except the quinces, to a large stainless steel saucepan and bring slowly to a boil to dissolve the sugar. Simmer for 2 minutes, then remove from the heat. Leave for 30 minutes to allow the aromatics to flavor the vinegar.

As quinces discolor quickly, prepare one fruit at a time. Peel, quarter, and core, then cut each quarter again in half or, depending on size, into thirds—aim for slices no more than ½-inch thick. Immediately drop into the vinegar. Cover with a disc of parchment paper and bring the vinegar back to a boil, then simmer for 30 minutes or until the fruit is tender when pierced with the tip of a sharp knife. Ladle into the warm sterilized jars (see page 132), seal tightly, and leave until cold before labeling and storing in the fridge until needed.

Place the ham hock in a deep saucepan—you need one big enough to allow the ham to be submerged in water. Add the veggies, herbs, and peppercorns, then cover the hock with cold water. Half cover the pan with a lid, bring to a boil over medium heat, then simmer for 2 to 2½ hours until the meat is very tender and starting to pull away from the bone. Remove from the heat and let cool in the liquid. Drain the ham, reserving ¾ cup of the poaching liquid.

Preheat the oven to 375°F. Line a roasting pan with a double thickness of foil.

Using a sharp knife, remove the skin from the ham hock, leaving a nice thick layer of fat, and stand upright in the lined roasting pan. Mix the mustard and honey together and slather it over the ham, then pour the reserved poaching liquid into the pan so that it comes no more than ½ inch up the sides of the ham. Bake on the middle rack for 30 to 40 minutes until well-glazed, basting two or three times during cooking. Lightly toast the walnuts on a baking sheet while the oven is on, then let the ham and nuts cool.

Put the watercress and radicchio in a large bowl. Place the oil, vinegar, and mustard in a canning jar, season well, screw on the lid, and shake well. Toss the salad leaves with enough dressing to coat, arrange on serving plates, and scatter with the toasted walnuts. Shred the ham into small bite-sized pieces and add to the salad. Finally, drain about 4 pickled quince slices per person and arrange on top. Scatter with the parsley and serve.

Index

Acknowledgments

Writing a book is never the work of just one person—there's a whole team of brilliantly talented people involved, without whom it would just be a jumble of words.

I feel incredibly lucky to write for Kyle Books, and can't thank Kyle enough for asking me to write another book—it seems a very long time ago that we had lunch at my kitchen table discussing this. My editor Judith Hannam really is one of the best and I thank my lucky stars every day that I get to work with her. Thank you for being so patient when my deadline was "looming" and when I went silent during my house move. And for indulging me yet again, with pages that are chock full of beautiful pictures, for putting together such a fantastic team, and for pulling everything together in your unflappable and gentle manner. Thank you also to Hannah Coughlin and Corinne Masciocchi for your meticulous double checking and proof-reading—eagle eyed the pair of you.

Yet again I have had the absolute pleasure to work with my great friend and brilliant photographer Tara Fisher. What you have bought to this book is beyond words. I have loved working with you for a few days at a time, every month for the 12 months that we worked on the photography—thank you my friend. Thank you to the best set-painter in town—Ms. Saskia Sierra—your choice of colors was spot on! And to Ms. Liliana Sierra who stood holding ice creams so perfectly for what must have felt like an eternity before we allowed her to actually eat one. And thanks to Sue Prescott for your brilliant re-touching and for keeping us sane and laughing.

To my wonderful assistant Kathryn Bruton, who is so much more than an assistant, you're a true friend, wonderful talent, and undisputed Queen of Soda Bread.

Miranda Harvey, whose incredibly beautiful design for this book really has bowled me over.

Mr. Mungo Jerry Boogaloo, who is getting increasingly stubborn with old age but thankfully will still accompany me on a good walk every day, just so long as we're going the way he wants to go and I have a pocket full of treats.

And finally to Hughie—thank you thank you thank you. *X*